# LEFT TURN, RIGHT TURN, U-TURN

# LEFT TURN, RIGHT TURN, U-TURN

The Return of the Prodigal Baby Boomers:
## OUR LAST CHANCE TO MAKE IT RIGHT

Angelo Paul Ramunni

*LEFT TURN, RIGHT TURN, U-TURN*
by Angelo Paul Ramunni

Printed in the United States of America

ISBN 9781613793657

www.xulonpress.com

# Table of Contents

# 1

## Somebody Has to Say It

*"Faith is to believe what you do not yet see; the reward for this faith is to see what you believe."*

~ Saint Augustine (354-430);
Roman Catholic saint

It had been a long time since I attended an Alcoholics Anonymous meeting. Not too long ago, a very good friend of mine called and asked me to come to his 35-year celebration. My friend had been sober for all of those 35 years, after spending the first half of his life abusing alcohol. That is no small accomplishment.

After our dinner, I sat toward the back of the room and watched as each participant of the AA program entered prior to the meeting. Something just didn't seem right to me, but I couldn't identify it right away. Just then the door opened and a very young looking man walked into the room, and that's when it hit me. Many of the people that were filing into the meeting were very young. In fact they were in their twenties! With well over 100 people in the room, it looked like any regular classroom full of college-aged students. How could this be? The average age of the people at the last AA meeting I went to seemed to be older, probably in their forties or fifties. When did all of this change?

After the meeting I asked my friend about this age shift.

1

He looked at me and said, "How long have we been hearing about the heavy drug traffic coming into our country? Tonight you saw a very small fraction of the people using those drugs. It's our youth, our children, who are losing their futures by becoming addicted to alcohol and drugs. The lucky ones are those that successfully make it through this program. But then they have a lifetime of struggle ahead of them to stay sober. And when you're as young as these folks it's even harder to accomplish that than it was for someone from my generation. They have young friends who like to drink and experiment with drugs, and their access to these drugs is virtually unlimited. These AA folks will be sorely tempted as they return to their families, friends and jobs. They will have a hard time staying sober."

For me, that AA meeting brought into focus something I had been thinking about for a long time. I am a member of what is commonly called the Baby Boomer generation. Those of us born between 1946 and 1964, give or take a few years, fall into that generational grouping. A great deal has changed in our culture over the last 60 years or so. To be sure, there are many good things that have been accomplished on our watch. However, when I see things like that AA meeting, or hear reports of teen suicide, teen pregnancy, abortion on demand, divorce rates hovering around 50%, and political corruption and dishonesty, it makes me wonder if we have done all that we can to help those who are younger than us learn how to live lives that are full, productive and honorable. Have we led them in the right direction? Have our lives been a good example of how best to live?

Let's look at it this way. Every day, more and more members of our generation approach retirement age. If we, as Baby Boomers, think of our life as being divided up into three sections, then we are about to enter into the last one-third of our lives. How do you want to live out the last one-third of your life? Are you planning to indulge yourself in things that you have always wanted to do? Do you feel you have earned your retirement through your many years of sacrifice and hard work, and no one is going to stop you from enjoying it? Or perhaps you will not be able to retire, and will still have to work your way through this last part of your life due to financial constraints.

In any event, this is it. This may be your last chance to plan a direction for the remaining part of your life. For some time now you may have been thinking that there is something special that you have yet to achieve. Do you know what needs to be done to accomplish your true purpose in life? Have you given any serious thought to what that purpose might be?

From time to time, polls are taken that ask people if we, as a nation, are headed in the right direction. Many respondents answer no, especially not these days. The reasons for such responses are usually numerous and oftentimes complicated. But they beg the question, if we are not headed in the right direction, then what is our best course of action? Well, we have a number of options. At the next opportunity or crossroads in our lives, we can either make a left hand turn or a right hand turn, or, for that matter, we could also just continue on the same wrong road heading in the same wrong direction. But the latter option might best fit a description of something Albert Einstein once said:

*The definition of insanity is continuing to do the same thing while expecting different results.*

Thankfully, a fourth option exists. We could choose to make a U-turn. We could decide to go back to the point where we turned off the right road and started down the wrong one. We could stop, re-check our map, and make sure we know for sure the right direction to take. Of course, this plan of action assumes that we have the right map, the right destination in mind, and that the destination is correct for us. After all, even if we are unsure of our course, wouldn't it still be wise to turn around?

Many Baby Boomers can remember the enthusiasm we had as we approached and entered our twenties. We were going to change the world. We were going to change the old ways of doing things that guaranteed the stale status quo of the 1960's and replace them with new ways that were more fair, compassionate, and beneficial to people. What happened? In short, many of us took a slight detour for the last 30 or 40 years to go to work, make money, raise a family, and enjoy life.

However, I'm willing to bet that old dream is still alive in many of us, even if it has been tempered by time. And perhaps now there is a sense of urgency in making that dream become a reality, if for no other reason than that we no longer have our whole lives in front of us to get it done. Instead, we know all too well that many of our good years are behind us now, and that time is passing very quickly.

Ironically, many of us have bought and invested heavily into the very same system we wanted to change. That system or way of life has changed, however, not necessarily because of our generational influence, but because of many other factors as well. Some would argue that it has changed mainly for the worse. Moreover, we are watching our children try to negotiate their way through that system of life, and it is not easy for them.

When I talk to people in their 50's and 60's, more often than not I get a feeling that they have not yet gained a personal sense of fulfillment in their lives despite, all their years of work and experience. Something big and important is still missing in their lives. Over the years we Boomers have always managed to attract the limelight to our causes and activities. As a generation, we have dominated the headlines in all walks of life. And it is reasonable to think that we are not yet finished. Our retirement years will most likely see a continuation of that trend.

That is why I have written this book. I am betting and hoping that we Boomers will now want to consider carefully whether we will *spend* the last part of our lives on ourselves or *invest* it in other people. There is a great difference between those two concepts. If we decide to spend the time we have left and what we have accumulated solely on ourselves, then we will probably continue down the same road we've been on all along. If we decide to invest it, then we will have to make a U-turn and question whom we should invest it in, and for what purpose?

In order to answer this last question, we would have to consider going back to times and places where we left things undone, and personally endeavor to make them right. The idea of going back to the place in our lives we were before we got distracted or sidelined is a good thought. We need to ask ourselves if there is someone we need to help or something we need to work on. Is there any unfinished business that we need to take care of that has been haunting us for years? Perhaps the opportunity to do the right thing is not behind us, but rather right in front of us, and we haven't yet been able to summon the courage to make the right choice or necessary commitment. Spending versus investing; these are two very different choices.

In the Bible, we learn the story of the Prodigal Son (Luke 15:11). Arguably, it is one of the most important stories in the entire Bible. It is the chronicle of a young man who takes his inheritance prematurely, leaves his father, his brother, and the security of home, and goes off to a far away city to indulge himself in every kind of pleasure. After some time passes, he becomes destitute, and is forced to reconsider his options. He decides to make a U-turn, a change of 180 degrees in his heading, and returns home. The story goes on to show that he made the right decision; upon his return, he immediately apologizes to his father, who, in turn, happily receives him, forgives him and restores all of his privileges as his son.

The decision to return, admit his mistake, and seek forgiveness was more than just the right choice. It essentially saved his life, not just in the here and now, but for all eternity.

It was the one correct option available to the young man and the one that his father anxiously wanted to see him choose. I wonder if we realize how important this story is for us today. Is it time for us, as individuals and as a generation, to take action similar to the one the son took in the story? Since the story of the Prodigal Son is extremely relevant for us today, we will discuss it in greater detail in a later chapter. In the meantime you might keep that story in the back of your mind as we continue.

Let's go a little further. Do you remember how Scrooge reacted to his visit from the three ghosts in Charles Dickens' *The Christmas Carol?* When Scrooge awoke on Christmas morning and found that he still had time to make things right, he was absolutely joyous. In a similar manner we should be elated that there still is time and opportunity left to make some real positive changes in our lives. I think that many of us in the Boomer generation are privately waking up to this realization. Time is growing short and there is much left to do.

We also need to realize that young people are looking to us to show them the correct way to live. They want to learn the lessons of our life experiences so that they don't make the same errors many of us older folks have made. Sadly, it seems as if all we have given our children is a wide-ranging menu of options as to how they can approach life's challenges. Relatively few of us older folks seem interested in showing them the right course to take, and, as a consequence, many of them are afraid of life.

I have been teaching at a local university for the last 14 years and I have seen a growing number of students who are afraid to make a commitment to getting married, choosing a career, purchasing a home, and having children. Instead, many are deferring decisions on making these commitments to a later part of their lives. They need us and our guidance. We need them, too, I believe, because part of the reason for our own existence as well as part of our current role in life is to give them that guidance.

So, somebody has to say it. Someone has to ask the questions: what is right and what is wrong? What's the best way to live? Does anyone know? Who can we turn to for an answer to these big questions? In the past, the answers would come from a source like the Bible. Not so long ago, most folks regarded the Scriptures as a definitive resource for discovering the truth and how we should let it guide us in living our lives. Even though, from a practical day-to-day point of view, many people would ignore the teachings found in the Bible, we still held it up to our children as the example for how they should determine right from wrong. For a rapidly growing portion of society, that no longer seems to be the case today.

We all know, for example, that when we are driving on a major highway and the posted speed limit is 55MPH, in reality that means we can do 65 or 70 MPH. Am I correct? Even the state police will probably not stop you if you keep your speed under 70MPH! So what is right and what is wrong in this case?

It matters a great deal to our children. They look to their parents, teachers, government officials and, in general, older people to *show* them what is right and wrong. Just from this one example, young people will extrapolate how they can behave in various other areas of life. If they can exceed posted speed limits and rules of the road then it follows that they can probably behave this way in other facets of their lives as well. So is this a problem or not? And if it is, whose responsibility is it to fix it?

I think it is *our* responsibility and our job as a generation to set the record straight. We need to make a big U-turn and set a new example for all to follow. We've got to tell our children what is right and wrong. We've got to tell them where we went wrong in our own lives and then show them by example how best to live from now on.

In many professions, there is a concept known as best practices. It is a series of actions, policies and procedures that professionals look to and employ in order to ensure the greatest success and return in their businesses. In this book, as we discuss some of the more relevant questions and issues of our day, I will rely on applying the notion of best practices to help give us real practical answers to these issues and questions.

For those of us wondering how faith in God plays a role in obtaining workable answers to life, there will also be numerous references to the Scriptures. This will illustrate how God's teachings can help to lead us in the right direction. You will be amazed at how many of life's best practices are in complete agreement with the Scriptures, and vice versa.

Consequently, you will notice very quickly that I rely quite heavily on the Scriptures for much of what I define as the truth. As I explain in a later chapter, I had to decide early on in writing this book what could possibly serve as a reliable and continuing source of truth. This is a big question: where could we turn on a consistent basis and be assured of getting the right answers to our questions? I reasoned that this source is either from within our world or from outside of it. In other words, it must be either a temporal source or a supernatural source.

The vast majority of people across the globe believe in a life beyond this one. Since this is what we believe to be true, it logically follows that there must be a supernatural being that supports and maintains the life to come (as well as this present one). That being must know what the real truth is; therefore it makes sense to rely on that being to teach us the real truth. I then had to choose one supernatural source out of all the options available to us, and I decided to choose Jesus Christ.

As a result of all of my studies and personal experiences with my Christian faith, I believe Jesus Christ to be the one true God. He is the only one of all our choices for a god that claims to have died for all of us, as well as for me. And I believe it. To believe otherwise would require me to take all of the events in my life, whether I had succeeded or failed or would have experienced serious pain or consequences, and account for all of the eventual positive outcomes as simply good luck and coincidence.

There were too many times, due to poor decisions or bad behavior, where I could have "cashed in my chips" or ended up as an invalid for the rest of my life (I was rather wild in my youth). At every turn something intervened on my behalf and to my benefit. Therefore, I know better than to question the existence of a benevolent force and something deep inside of me still strongly confirms that feeling today.

Another thought encouraged me to write this book: I think when God created us, He did not mean for us to have such a difficult time in living our lives. I believe he intended for us to exist in something of a paradise. When I see advertisements for vacation spots in places with lush landscapes, warm climates, beautiful beaches and a carefree existence, I think that's the kind of life that God had in mind for us.

Something happened to ruin all of that. What that something was, and continues to be, is sin. I can accept this as a reason. But does that mean we cannot change that? Is there some way we older folks, in the time we have left, could gather together and to help restore at least some of that original vision and dream for those younger than us? I think there is. That is what this book is all about: the restoration of the original vision God had for us all. However, in order to accomplish this dream, many of us will have to make a personal U-turn.

In case you have not yet realized it, "U-turn" is a contemporary way of expressing the word "repent." We need to repent of our bad habits and actions. We need to change our ways, apologize to those we have hurt, and make restitution where necessary. We need to move in a new direction away from our old ways.

The U-turn starts with us mentally assenting to the new direction. It must make logical sense to us and we must realize that it is high time for the move. So the new direction we are contemplating is first agreed to in a very cerebral (head-level, instead of heart-level) manner.

Then we must become almost obsessive about our U-turn. It starts to makes so much sense to us that we become passionately involved in making it happen. We therefore become invested in the process at the heart level. Lastly, and most importantly, the commitment has to move into our gut area. It has to evoke a visceral feeling, telling us "I've just got to do this." In fact, once we get to this point, we cannot eat, drink, sleep, work, etc unless we go through with the change. It becomes a mission for us. It literally changes our behavior. If we can hold onto all three areas of control, the head, the heart and the gut, then we have a good chance of success. Of course the whole process has to be bathed in prayer, regular and fervent prayer, because without God's help, we will not succeed.

> *I am the vine; you are the branches. If a man remains in me and I in him, he will bear much fruit; apart from me you can do nothing.* (John 15:5, emphasis added)

The questions I am posing to the Boomer generation are: how will you spend the last third of your life? Do you owe anyone anything? If you could, what past events would you like to change? If you had to do it over again, would you make the same choices? Are there any relationships in your past, and even today, that need to be repaired or improved? If the people you need to talk to are now gone, can you transfer your desire to make it right to the people who are now in your life? Do you have any grandchildren that need to learn what is right and what is wrong? Can they gain from your life experiences?

Perhaps none of these questions apply to your situation. Perhaps you are just beginning to grasp the fact that you have yet to reach your full potential, and that you need to finally realize your true purpose in life. Perhaps you are intrigued with the notion that all of us together could still make things better, even though much in life today seems to be broken. Just as it was when we were all young and idealistic, we still have another opportunity to change things for the better. But time is running out. This may be our last chance.

We are currently at one of our generation's last major crossroads. Many of us are at the point of making choices about our retirement. As I said, we could simply take a left-hand turn or we could also choose to take a right-hand turn. For that matter we could just keep going in the same direction we are heading right now. But we might need to consider taking a bigger and more permanent step. With all of the things we experience every day that are not right in our lives, it makes sense to think about turning around and heading back. Both the Prodigal Son and Scrooge did the same thing in their respective stories and it worked out wonderfully for them.

Both the Prodigal Son and Scrooge eventually came to the conclusion that they were lost and needed to find their "home base" again. We too have strayed far from our "home base," which is in many ways represented by the core values and basic Christian principles that have served generation after generation so well. Are we ready to give them up for good? Or should we do all that we can in the time we have left to reclaim them for ourselves and our children?

At the end of this book, we will be left with a choice. The choice is to either keep going in the direction we are headed and hope everything will work out okay, or to stop and consider going back. If we make that U-turn and decide to go back, we will become "restorers." Our job will be to fix, repair and do what we can to restore relationships and people to good health.

In fact, this whole book is about restoration. Just as Christ came to restore our relationship with God, we can decide to do the same thing with one another. His example would be a good place to start and is a good model for us to follow.

I'll end this chapter with a serious question: if a young person asked your opinion as to the best ways to live his or her life, what would you say? Would you be ready with a good answer?

How would you begin to answer that question? Where would you get the information to answer him or her? Think about this as we go further. I am asked these questions very often, in one form or another, by my students at college. If you cannot come up with a good answer, then it may be time for you to consider what's involved in making a U-turn. Are you ready to consider taking that step?

If so, then read on...

*This is what the LORD says:*
*Stand at the crossroads and look;*
*ask for the ancient paths,*
*ask where the good way is, and walk in it,*
*and you will find rest for your souls.*    (Jeremiah 6:16)

*"What is uttered from the heart alone, will win the hearts of others to your own."*

~ Johann Wolfgang von Goethe (1749-1832);
philosopher, scientist, author

# 2

## Revelation, Discovery, Signs and Wonders

*"People are like stained-glass windows. They sparkle and shine when the sun is out, but when the darkness sets in, their true beauty is revealed only if there is a light from within."*

~ Elisabeth Kübler-Ross (1926-2004);
psychiatrist, author

It was twenty years ago in early 1990 when I found myself at a low point in my life. I was very tired of the work I was doing as a CPA in public practice. It seemed that all I did for people was to just fill out government forms and try to file them in a timely manner. I was not providing any kind of real long-lasting service that could help people live better lives. In truth, I was searching for something that was missing from my life, but I really didn't know what it was at the time. I had a wonderful wife and two young children, a nice home and I wanted for nothing. In theory, my life was everything I had hoped and planned for. But still, it did not feel complete; something big had to be missing.

From a spiritual perspective, I have been a Catholic all my life. But up until 20 years ago my approach to matters of faith lacked passion and a desire to know more. I had become a "mechanical Catholic" going through the routines of church membership, attending Mass, and taking Communion, all while being on auto-pilot. Then, in April of 1990, I came across a book called *In His Steps* by Charles Sheldon. It was written about 100 years earlier and it asked the critical question: "What would Jesus do?" In other words, if Jesus was in my shoes every day, how would He respond to all the various challenges and events that occurred?

I had never heard that question asked before, much less gave it any thought. To me, Jesus was very busy and had no time to notice someone as insignificant as me. But the question stuck in my mind and I could not shake it loose. Before long, I was asking that question in relation to a variety of things I encountered on a personal and professional level, and it started to change my life. I began to realize that my concept of Jesus as being too distant or busy to notice me and care about me personally could not be more incorrect. In fact, the exact opposite was true then and is still true today.

This new insight turned my world upside down. I liken it to being a mathematician all of your life and believing that 2 + 2 = 5. Suddenly, one day you find out that the correct answer is 4! You now realize that everything you did as a mathematician for all of those years was in error. That is how I felt after I had the revelation that Christ wanted a close personal relationship with me. Now I was "on fire," as they say, and I could not get enough of the Scriptures into my mind and heart. The more I read the deeper I fell in love with Jesus Christ.

The result of this epiphany was a book I wrote and self-published in 2005 entitled *The Poor Catholic; The Road to Grace.* In it I explained what it meant to be a poor Catholic: someone who is missing the most important thing in life, a close and personal friendship with Jesus. In the book, the poor Catholic actually was me. I was and still am the original poor Catholic. Some people told me the title should have instead been *The Poor Christian* because people of all Christian denominations suffer from the same lack of a meaningful relationship with Jesus on a personal level.

In the book, I recall growing up watching many people come into church Sunday after Sunday and purposely sitting or standing in the rear of the church. It was if they were afraid to get closer to God by sitting in the front pews. Jesus said to us:

> *Do not let your hearts be troubled. Trust in God; trust also in me. In my Father's house are many rooms; if it were not so, I would have told you. I am going there to prepare a place for you. And if I go and prepare a place for you, I will come back and take you to be with me that you also may be where I am. You know the way to the place where I am going.* (John 14:1-4)

A poor Catholic or Christian is someone who does not realize that all of the blessings, healings and other things we need most are deep inside our Lord's mansion. If we stay out in the front hallway, or in the last rows of pews, we will miss out on all of the blessings He has for us inside, and that will guarantee our poorness. Therefore, the choice is ours: keep your distance from God and remain poor, or come into His home and enjoy what He has for each of us. We become rich in His love the closer we get to Him and the more attention we pay to Him.

Imagine a person going to his mother's house for the usual Sunday meal. He enters the house, puts a chair just inside the front door, and sits there with his coat on for just a short while because he really has to get going pretty soon. His mother sees him there and says "What are you doing out here? Come inside, your sister and brother are here with their kids and uncle Joe has joined us too. Why are you sitting in the hallway?" Wouldn't

16

that be a crazy thing to do? Wouldn't your mother and other relatives be offended? Wouldn't you miss out on the food, the laughter, the news about the family, all of the good stuff? Everyone else would miss you and feel like you really were not there. Why would you go to your mother's house if you did not really want to spend time with her and the others?

But that is exactly what many of us do in God's house every Sunday morning and, for that matter, every day of the week. We make a serious, and, in many cases, a conscious effort at keeping our distance from Him. Why do we do this? It will truly make us poor in every sense of the word. No wonder we are all feeling over-burdened, exhausted and fed up with life. Many of us treat God like we do our local fire department or ambulance squad. We only want Him to intervene in our lives when we are in serious trouble, thinking we can otherwise handle things well enough on our own.

Growing up as a Catholic felt like more of a corporate experience than a personal one for me. Everything I did at church happened with many other people present, particularly when it came to the sacraments. I never got the notion that Christ was someone who wanted to walk with just me and help me through my personal issues. I too used to "hang out" in the rear of the church each Sunday. I was afraid to get close to the altar and to Him.

The only time I would get close to Him was when I had to go to confession. But then He was like the stern father figure that came home from work every day and wanted a report as to how bad I had been. The only time He ever seemed to talk to me was in the confessional, to tell me how much penance I had to do for my sinful behavior. I never had the feeling that He wanted to hear about any of the good things I had accomplished.

I made sure that the theme of our being aloof from Jesus

came through loud and clear in my first book. Many people who read it reported that they had had very similar experiences. The following message appeared on the back cover of *The Poor Catholic; The Road to Grace:*

*So, you were born a Catholic and baptized into the Catholic church. You made your first communion and received your confirmation. You were married in the Catholic church and raised your children as Catholics. You went to church most Sundays and holy days and even went to confession. You supported your church financially. And now you just had a beautiful Catholic funeral and you fully expect to enter Heaven.*
*Are you really sure that God will let you in?*

After it was published and sales increased, I started to get very revealing comments from different people. Interestingly and most unexpectedly, a good deal of the mail and discussion came from men. I can generalize and sum it up this way: most of the men (and some of the women) who responded reminded me a great deal of the Prodigal Son parable. They knew they had strayed far from God over a period of many years. They had become involved in unethical financial deals, acquired addictive behaviors, and involved themselves in things that, if known publicly, would cost them their jobs, their marriages and their standing in the community. Some of those who spoke to me even indicated that what they had done (and in some cases were still doing) was outright illegal.

In short, it became obvious that these troubled people were carrying the burden of a great deal of private sin. They were in the same situation as the Prodigal Son who went off to taste and experience all that the world had to offer. The difference was that when the Prodigal Son's mistakes finally broke him, he had enough sense to make his way back home and ask his father for forgiveness.

However, the people I had been speaking to were afraid to "come home." If they did, they would have to confess as to where they had been and what they had been doing. Actually, the easy part would be confessing to a priest or pastor in a church confessional setting. The impossibly hard part would be to confess to their spouses, families, friends, business partners, IRS, and everyone else. For many, the price they would have to pay to "come clean" would be too expensive. They therefore remain in their poor spiritual state, prisoners of their sins and past actions with no way to effectively come home again. They are indeed poor Catholics, poor Christians and poor people in every sense. Their actions have put them into a veritable private prison cell.

Despite these revelations, I continued to give seminars and talks in and outside of churches to groups of individuals and Christian business owners. We worked through the concept of "what would Jesus do" and related it to many different everyday real-life situations. These sessions seemed to work, at first, but after a while I noticed that the same people kept meeting, praying and discussing the same tough issues and questions. Something was missing. For some reason, people were not having the kind of *permanent* spiritual breakthrough that could manifest itself in a real way in their lives. It became more and more obvious to me that something very important had yet to be addressed.

As I said, the revelation that I had over 20 years ago that Jesus wanted a close personal walking relationship with me was an enormous event in my life. Yet as I settled into that notion and became comfortable with it on an intellectual level, I realized that He was not only going to talk to me and treat me as a friend, but He was also going to ask me to help Him do certain things that He wanted done. He tested me constantly as I learned what He taught me. It did not take me long to realize that being a true Christian and following in Christ's footsteps was the most difficult task a person could undertake.

As time went on, it became more and more difficult for me to comply with His requests on a daily basis. Having an intimate relationship with the God of the universe is an incredible experience, but it is very overwhelming, to say the least. As with any relationship there is always a give and take. With Jesus, I have come to find that He does expect a great deal from us, particularly by our earthly standard of friendship. But He also offers us something that no one else can give: the incomparable gift of eternal life.

Eventually, the strain on my personal relationship with God, coupled with the failure that I and others in my prayer groups were experiencing in successfully applying our faith to serious life issues, drove me to ask God for another revelation. I asked Him to show me what was missing. I asked him why we weren't having the kind of breakthrough spiritual experiences we read about in the Bible and elsewhere. And I believe He has answered me.

Allow me to explain it to you as He did for me. The following are two very chilling pieces of Scripture that for many years I never fully understood, or, for that matter, wanted to understand. Now I think I finally see what He is telling us. The first one comes from the Book of Matthew:

> *Not everyone who says to me, 'Lord, Lord,' will enter the*
> *kingdom of heaven, but only he who does the will of my*
> *Father who is in heaven. Many will say to me on that*

*day, 'Lord, Lord, did we not prophesy in your name, and in your name drive out demons and perform many miracles?' Then I will tell them plainly, 'I never knew you. Away from me, you evildoers!'* (Matthew 7:21-23)

The second one also is found in Matthew:

*At that time the disciples came to Jesus and asked, "Who is the greatest in the kingdom of heaven?"*
*He called a little child and had him stand among them. And he said: "I tell you the truth, unless you change and become like little children, you will never enter the kingdom of heaven. Therefore, whoever humbles himself like this child is the greatest in the kingdom of heaven. And whoever welcomes a little child like this in my name welcomes me. But if anyone causes one of these little ones who believe in me to sin, it would be better for him to have a large millstone hung around his neck and to be drowned in the depths of the sea."* (Matthew 18:1-6)

These verses have troubled me very much over the years because they describe people who are already working with and for God. In the first example, people are performing what we would call miracles today. How could God find fault with the people who did this amazing work? In the second example, Jesus speaks these words to the Disciples themselves. The inference is that if a person does anything that leads a young person or a person new to the Christian faith to sin, he will be condemned forever!

Matthew 18:1-6 describes not only the active commission of sin but also the kind of sin committed when someone fails to take action to *prevent* a sin from occurring. Clearly, Jesus was talking about and expecting a level of compliance from us that seems to be far beyond our ability to achieve.

After a good deal of intensive study, I have learned that what God is telling us is that, above all, He wants us to have such a close personal relationship with Him that nothing else will compete and distract us from Him. First and foremost, we should always make certain that the personal connection we have with Him is strong and functional. Why is that so important? It is the only way we can be prevented from going off on our own, even for just a short while, to perform a work (even for Him) on our own strength and knowledge. Those are the times when we can be most vulnerable to sin. That was whom he described in Matthew 7:21-23: people who were essentially doing their own thing in God's name.

Our connection to Christ has to be complete and we must stay connected 100% of the time. Without His constant support and protection, gaps occur and we can be led off the right road, and possibly lead others to sin as well. We do not want to be guilty of committing that sin as it will inevitably have disastrous consequences for us. I liken it to driving a car. We have to be watchful and attentive at all times. We cannot take our eyes off the road for even a second. So when His Disciples tried to prevent the little children from seeing Him, He responded with rather harsh words as we see in the Matthew 18 verse.

After my research on these verses, I now had a clue as to what might be missing in our relationship with Jesus. Our connection was not complete. Many of us will look for God, find Him and stay with Him for a while. We will then leave Him to do what we feel we need to do, promising that we will soon return. In that interim, we are at great risk of committing sin. We are at risk because we have disconnected from Him in order to do the thing(s) we wanted. We feel we can handle whatever it is on our own.

Even if we go off "to do God's work", it is very easy to fall into the trap of doing that work on our own power, not through the power of His Holy Spirit and by His instruction. To put it simply, trying to fit God into our schedule only at times that are convenient for us will not work. I have found that it is best not to try to book God into my schedule or ask for a meeting only in certain times of need. That arrangement does not work. He wants to be with us all the time; He works best under those conditions. As He said *"...without me you can do nothing."* (John 15:5) He wants us to be spiritually monogamous and connected to Him at all times. For us, the deal can't be beat . He's on call 24/7/365 and does not sleep!

Look at this Scripture:

*As they were walking along the road, a man said to him, "I will follow you wherever you go." Jesus replied, "Foxes have holes and birds of the air have nests, but the Son of Man has no place to lay his head." He said to another man, "Follow me." But the man replied, "Lord, first let me go and bury my father." Jesus said to him, "Let the dead bury their own dead, but you go and proclaim the kingdom of God." Still another said, "I will follow you, Lord; but first let me go back and say good-by to my family." Jesus replied, "No one who puts his hand to the plow and looks back is fit for service in the kingdom of God."*

(Luke 9:57-62)

23

These verses are speaking directly to would-be followers of Christ and emphasizing how important their mission would be in the eyes of God. Once undertaken, the work of being a real Christian supersedes everything else... everything. The requests made by the people speaking to Jesus in these verses seem reasonable to us because they represent how we are accustomed to living each day. We perform our work in increments and steps, one thing after another. But for the kind of task Jesus has for His followers, that kind of approach will not work.

We have to be ready to put 100% of ourselves into whatever He asks and to do it when he requires it be done. For us, it is a duty as for the fire department or ambulance crew I cited earlier. When the alarm rings, the responders must drop whatever they are doing and respond to the call.

Nonetheless, this revelation proved to be too much for me during my struggles. At the time, I was not ready to accept as truth the overwhelming commitment that was demanded of me. I thought maybe if I prayed more, read the Scriptures more, talked with other Christians more, attended Christian seminars, retreats and conferences more, and went to church more, I would be closer to Him and satisfy His requirements. It soon became obvious, though, that these efforts would also fail to answer my question.

Then it happened. I finally discovered what many of us have been missing all of this time  and that discovery convinced me I had to put pen to paper in order to tell others about what I have found to be true: we must make a U-turn. We must repent.

When John The Baptist heralded the arrival of the Christ, his message was singular in its meaning: he simply told us to repent. He told us to make straight our paths and to ask for forgiveness of our sins. When Jesus came out of the desert after 40 days of fasting and prayer, His first message was the same as John's: repent. I suddenly realized that we have been trying to serve God in order to stay with Him but at the same time keeping some of our favorite sinful habits. We're acting like the person who promises to love, honor, obey and cherish their spouse but continues to have a secret relationship with a former lover.

We go to church, we pray, we go to Christian conferences, we donate to charities. But we continue to cherish some of our old habits which are contrary to God's laws. We will readily acknowledge our sinful behavior to Him, but at the same time we justify the need to continue these practices both to ourselves and to God. We cannot bear the thought of going cold turkey without our sinful crutches. We promise God that we just need a little more time to get rid of the habit, but that does not work.

Keeping our sinful habits while trying to work for the Lord will cripple us. It will turn us into invalids because we are always in a state of conflict and turmoil within ourselves, fighting against our conscience and God. If we want to repent, if we want the U-turn to be successful, we must do it and not look back. We must stay on the new course.

Many of us have much in common with the rich young ruler in Luke, Chapter 18, as the following verses show.

*A certain ruler asked him, "Good teacher, what must I*
*do to inherit eternal life?"*
*"Why do you call me good?" Jesus answered. "No one is*
*good — except God alone. You know the*
*commandments: 'Do not commit adultery, do not*
*murder, do not steal, do not give false testimony, honor*
*your father and mother.'"*
*"All these I have kept since I was a boy," he said.*

*When Jesus heard this, he said to him, "You still lack one thing. Sell everything you have and give to the poor, and you will have treasure in heaven. Then come, follow me." When he heard this, he became very sad, because he was a man of great wealth. Jesus looked at him and said, "How hard it is for the rich to enter the kingdom of God! Indeed, it is easier for a camel to go through the eye of a needle than for a rich man to enter the kingdom of God."*

(Luke 18:18-25)

This passage describes so accurately the condition of many of us in the present day. Note that the person in question is rich, and tries to justify his lavish lifestyle to Jesus. He wanted personal assurance from God that it is acceptable to pursue wealth, along with all of the kinds of pleasures a wealthy person enjoys, as long as he complies with some of the more common rules of the faith. In fact, he wanted to know that he could still gain eternal life despite his earthly pursuits.

These passages reveal what it means to be a true Christian, a real follower of Jesus Christ. They mean that we have to be ready to give up all that we have in this world, especially the things we cherish the most, the things that have the greatest grip on us and the things that take up most of our attention. In this case the young ruler could not let go of his money; it had too strong a grip on him and it was what prevented him from having a real personal relationship with Christ. And he knew it. He had to choose between Christ and his way of life, and he chose the latter.

God's work is much more important than our everyday jobs. He is trying to save us for all eternity. Most of us are primarily concerned with making money to support ourselves financially.

While that is an important and necessary focus, in the bigger picture we must realize that this life will eventually end, and we will face the question of our disposition for all eternity. Over the (eternal) long run, which job is more important?

Jesus told this rich man and all who would listen that one cannot "rent your relationship with God." In order for God to work effectively in our lives, our interaction with God cannot be on-again, off-again. When we think about this, it does make sense. If we get a prescription for medication from a doctor, don't we take the dosage on a regular and consistent basis every day? If we don't, the medicine will not be effective. When we accept a job, we work for that employer 100% and we dedicate ourselves to our work. The same applies to marriage or any business partnership. We need to work at it 100% of the time with 100% of our strength and resources, or it is subject to the increased probability that it will fail.

As I came to discover these truths, I realized that this is what we might call a "supreme best practice." When it comes to matters of faith, many of us think that we can give God a portion of our time and attention and that He will be happy with that part alone. But much in life works in exactly the opposite way. Consider all of the major league baseball players, golfers and others that achieve high levels of success. Actually you can take the entire world of sports and use it as an example of what we are discussing here. All of the most successful players put 100% of themselves into their game in order to be the best they can be at their sport.

God wants us to be as close to Him as possible so we can be as successful as possible in the work we do for Him. But the pursuit of the answer I was looking for did not end here. I found that I had to "drill down" even further into God's Word in order to get at the real answers I wanted. I next had to find out *why*

God wants us to be so close to Him.

Many of the themes in the Bible have to do with repentance. Because it seems to be such an important personal issue for Jesus, I decided that I needed to study it further. It also happens to be the key to the issues presented in this book.

True and complete repentance comprises a number of components, including sorrow for our transgression, an admission of guilt, an apology to the wronged party, a desire to repair the damage done, a complete change in our thinking and a full turning of 180 degrees away from the sinful behavior that got us into trouble in the first place. We have to resolve to give up bad habits, not sort of, not kind of, or at some future date, but right now. And we cannot return to them ever again.

It is very much like Alcoholics Anonymous or any other drug rehab program. Once you enter the program to get rid of your addiction, you can never go back to that drug. That is the only way to regain your total health. In other words, we need to make a permanent and final U-turn with regard to the issue in question. And therein lies the problem. Many of us are not willing to give up all of our sinful habits completely, yet we still want to serve the Lord. We want the best of both worlds; we want it all.

But as Jesus said:

> *No servant can serve two masters. Either he will hate the one and love the other, or he will be devoted to the one and despise the other. You cannot serve both God and Money.* (Luke 16:13)

This has been our problem. Many of us are trying to have both a close personal relationship with Jesus Christ and a close personal relationship with our favorite sinful habit. It does not work that way and cannot ever work that way. God and sin are completely incompatible. They are mutually exclusive.

*Seek the LORD while he may be found; call on him while he is near.* (Isaiah 55:6)

*Then Jesus told them, "You are going to have the light just a little while longer. Walk while you have the light, before darkness overtakes you. The man who walks in the dark does not know where he is going. Put your trust in the light while you have it, so that you may become sons of light."* (John 12:35-36)

These verses speak to a coming time of separation from God. We still have Him as this is being written. But the level of sin in our world has become so great that eventually God will leave us to our sin and its consequences. Judgment will occur. While that may sound harsh, that is how we live our lives every day. We must bear the consequences of wrong living and bad choices. God never leaves us but we leave Him to do our own thing, just as the Prodigal Son left his father. He created the distance between himself and his dad and he paid the consequences.

This point also helps explain who those people were in the Scripture verses of Matthew 7:21. They were walking with God and even performing miracles in His name but they kept Him at arms length because of their personal sin. They were not completely connected to Him. Their relationship was not at the 24/7/365 level.

It is this disconnect, I believe, that is the answer as to why many of us still struggle with the same issues over and over again even though we have prayed and appealed to God on many occasions. Real spiritual breakthrough and an effective relationship with God can occur only when we commit to Christ 100%. Nothing short of that will do. Hanging onto that which we know is sinful in God's eyes cripples us and damages our relationship with Him. Our sin will grieve Him, and the distance between us and God will grow. It may appear that God is leaving us, but He is not. We in fact are leaving Him, little by little. Sin is an abductor and it works just like any other perpetrator of abduction. It endeavors to take us far from the One who could save us.

Trying to keep both Jesus and our sinful behavior will never work. Think of it this way: can you imagine telling your spouse right after your wedding day that you have a couple of close old friends that you would like to keep seeing on a romantic basis? How do you think your spouse would react? Enough said? The mutual exclusivity of God and sin happens to be a pivotal issue both for this book as well as for all of us who claim to be Christians. If we fail to understand this issue, we will fail as Christians.

As Christians, we believe that when Jesus went to the cross to atone for our sins, it was the most critical moment in all of history, past, present and future. There can be no more important moment than that one; Christ suffered for us because of our sins, those which had separated us from God. The distance between us and God was enormous. We therefore needed someone to intervene for us to repair the breech in our relationship with God. No one human could bridge the gap. It had to be someone special, someone who was blameless in the sight of God, and that someone had to be Jesus. There was no one else who had the capacity to achieve our goal of unity with God again.

God cannot live with sin. He banished Adam and Eve from the Garden because of it. Prior to that, He walked with them and was intimate with them in the Garden. But Adam and Eve gave up their relationship with God when they chose to break His law and eat the forbidden fruit. In the Old Testament, animal sacrifice is as an acceptable way to absolve sin from the Israelites. In a like manner, someone had to be the sacrificial (lamb) go-between for us. Christ had to intervene on our behalf before God the Father. This is something we cannot fully understand right now. Perhaps in the next life it will become clear.

You may remember this chilling passage:

> *At the sixth hour darkness came over the whole land until the ninth hour. And at the ninth hour Jesus cried out in a loud voice, "Eloi, Eloi, lama sabachthani?", which means, "My God, my God, why have you forsaken me?"* (Mark 15:33-34)

We Christians have heard these words many times in church, in particular during Easter, but how many of us know what was happening to Jesus at this moment? Yes, He was dying and the physical pain was unimaginable. Yet something even more painful and frightening was occurring to Him: He was being separated from His Father. When Jesus took the sins of the world on His shoulders, God the Father could not look upon His Son.

Sin is that repulsive to God. Jesus, for the first time ever, experienced what it was like to be separated from His Father, as a result of our sin.

This point cannot be overstated. Some in our culture these days think that sin, both as a concept and in reality, was something that only occurred to people in the past. They feel that it is a part of or a component to our history. But for us today, it no

31

longer relates to modern-day lifestyles and therefore does not concern us on a personal level. If there is a God and if He will someday judge us, we believe that He will overlook most, if not all of our sin and allow us into Paradise to be with Him. But my main point is this: if God could allow and sanction the death of His only son because of our sin that He took on himself, can we logically expect Him to be more generous and forgiving to us in the end? Sin separates anyone and anything from God.

Jesus experienced what we experience. When we sin, a dis-connect from the Father occurs. Remember, the Trinity has no beginning or end. God the Father, the Son and the Holy Spirit just "are." That is exactly what God said to Moses through the story of the burning bush in Exodus. The same can also be said for Jesus. God the Father, God the Son and God the Holy Spirit had never been separated from one another before that day on the cross.

That is why Jesus cried out in agony. He, for the first time ever, felt the loss of His Father, even though it would only be for a short while. Three verses later in verse 37, Jesus gives up His spirit and dies. When Jesus asked *"My God, my God, why have you forsaken me?"* He did not do so out of despair or a sud-den loss of confidence in God. Rather it is believed that He was quoting Psalm 22 as written by King David many years earlier as David predicted the agony and death of the Messiah:

> *My God, my God, why have you forsaken me?*
> *Why are you so far from saving me,*
> *so far from the words of my groaning?*      (Psalm 22:1)

Jesus was aware that as soon as He took on all of our sins, they would act to separate Him from His Father. The separation would be a temporary one but nevertheless, the prospect of being unable to commune with His Father even for a short while was almost unbearable even for Jesus. I never realized, until a few years ago, that when Jesus was agonizing in the Garden of Gethsemane before He was arrested, His grief was not solely for the physical pain and torture that He was about to endure. For certain, that was to be a terrible thing. But rather, it was the spiritual isolation from God that He would have to bear that brought Him so much trepidation and fear. It was so great that He even asked God to reconsider and spare him this unthinkable agony.

*Going a little farther, he fell to the ground and prayed that if possible the hour might pass from him. "Abba, Father," he said, "everything is possible for you. Take this cup from me. Yet not what I will, but what you will."*
(Mark 14:35-36)

As we know, in the end Jesus submitted to the will of God the Father and went to the cross for us. What I believe very few people understand and appreciate is that Jesus could not bear the thought of being separated from His Father, even for a short while. What does this signify for our relationship with God? Can we continue to treat our connection to God as an on-again, off-again relationship? Is it as simple as flipping a light switch on or off? I think not.

Again, the Trinity of God the Father, the Son and the Holy Spirit, has been present for all of eternity. They have no beginning or end. God allowed something to occur, within the confines of our earthly existence and bound by the constrictions of time and space, that would forever affect the reality of God's eternal world. He allowed and sanctioned the death of Jesus Christ, His only son. He allowed Jesus to be separated from Him, God the Father. That is just an unthinkable, unfathomable and truly unimaginable act. As Christians, these tenets are what we believe in our theology and our daily walk with God, and are critically important to understand. We will revisit them in a later chapter.

Sin is the cause of all our problems today. Until we give up our sinful behavior, we will remain hostage to the effects of sin. Sin is like cancer. The goal of cancer is to destroy the human body in this life. However, the ultimate goal of sin is to destroy us for all eternity. Perhaps after this discussion we may have a better understanding of what our sin has done to us and continues to do to our relationship with God today. Nothing other than sin can hurt Him more. In order to be real Christians, we must stop sinning. At the very least, when we realize that we have sinned, we must immediately turn to our Father and ask for forgiveness.

The U-turn we have to make must be swift and complete. Anything that separates us from God for any length of time must be avoided at all costs. In fact, if it is at all humanly possible, we must go back and fix what we have done wrong in the past, as well as what we are doing in the present. Just because we have moved forward from whatever it was that we did wrong years ago, and put it behind us, God will still hold us accountable for those wrongs. We have probably hurt others, and He wants those others to be healed because they will not heal on their own. The wounds will fester and be the source of continued hatred and animosity, poisoning the lives of those injured. These wounds will lead them and those around them to sin. Can we live with that on our conscience?

In some cases, we may be the ones that were hurt. If we are the wronged party and we suffered because of someone else's greed or error, it is our responsibility to hold them accountable for it. These wrongs must be righted, to the degree that we have any power to right them, for the same reason. We will carry with us the seeds of animosity and hate toward those who hurt us, making us bitter and angry. We may not think we are affected or that we are over it, but chances are that those feelings lie deep within us and will emerge in another form at another time. The wrongs could very well poison future relationships and cause us and those around us to sin. Additionally God wants to see us repair the wrong, not for the purpose of vengeance or for our personal gain, but because that lingering sin will create a barrier between God and the sinner, and that barrier will remain until forgiveness is sought.

What follows is one of the most difficult pieces of Scripture ever written:

> *Therefore, if you are offering your gift at the altar and there remember that your brother has something against you, leave your gift there in front of the altar. First go and be reconciled to your brother; then come and offer your gift.* (Matt 5:23-24)

Jesus Himself reinforces this point. He doesn't even want our gifts of money, talent, time or anything else unless we are first at peace with our neighbor; then we can therefore be at peace with Him. For a human being, harboring unrepentant sin is equivalent to committing eternal suicide. What could be worse than that?

Growing up as a Catholic, I always remember how impor-tant it was for us to go to confession before we could receive

Communion at Mass. I noticed that not everyone would get up to receive the host. I'd say to myself "I guess those folks haven't gone to confession recently." Nowadays in many Catholic churches, many folks go to Communion, but hardly anyone is going to confession. What does that do to us?

Listen to these words from First Corinthians:

> *Therefore, whoever eats the bread or drinks the cup of the Lord in an unworthy manner will be guilty of sinning against the body and blood of the Lord. A man ought to examine himself before he eats of the bread and drinks of the cup. For anyone who eats and drinks without recognizing the body of the Lord eats and drinks judgment on himself. That is why many among you are weak and sick, and a number of you have fallen asleep. But if we judged ourselves, we would not come under judgment. When we are judged by the Lord, we are being disciplined so that we will not be condemned with the world.* (1 Corinthians 11:27-32. Emphasis added)

Just take a moment and think about what these words are telling us. On the surface, going to Communion may seem like a good thing. However, if we do not first check ourselves for sin before God, and yet go to receive Him in Communion, we may actually be doing more harm than good to ourselves. This is another great example of what damage we do if we try to hang onto our sinful behavior while attempting to walk with the Lord. It does not work, and by our actions we add to our sickness and troubles.

In summary, the supreme best practice for having a successful relationship with Christ is to eliminate all sin from your life.

Being human we cannot be perfect all the time. We therefore have the fallback position of God's grace, which is always there to catch us if and when we fall. But we must want that grace; God will never force it on anyone. We must use our free will to ask for His grace, His forgiveness and His love, and we must accept it when it comes.

Real spiritual breakthrough can and will occur when we want it so badly that we ask for it in prayer, look for it expectantly and embrace it totally when it comes. Connecting with Christ and then breaking that connection with willful sin, and then coming back to connect again does not work. It is a risky ploy born of ignorance and one that cannot succeed with God. Forgiveness is always there for us, as is His grace. But our purpose must be to stay connected 100% of the time with God. Anytime we "pull the plug" and go off to do our thing, we put ourselves at great risk. Always remember the agony Christ suffered in the Garden of Gethsemane. The Son of God was in great distress because of the pending separation He would experience from His Father. If Jesus could barely tolerate the pain, what would eternal separation from God mean for us?

The great revelation and discovery I made about our relationship with God resides in how we were designed and constructed. As Adam and Eve were originally built to be in constant contact with God, we too are built to be with our Lord in constant spiritual union. We were made that way because that is what God intended. I now see that many of the problems we encounter every day are due in large part to our willfully connecting and disconnecting from God. We are the modern day version of prodigal sons and daughters, many of whom return to our Father for what we need but then, after some time, we leave again and go back to what has gotten us into trouble in the first place. That is the worst road to be on. We need to turn around and go back now and remain there.

*"Gratitude unlocks the fullness of life. It turns what we have into enough, and more. It turns denial into acceptance, chaos to order, confusion to clarity. It can turn a meal into a feast, a house into a home, a stranger into a friend. Gratitude makes sense of our past, brings peace for today and creates a vision for tomorrow. "*

~ Melodie Beattie;
motivational author

# 3

## Why Do We Have to Make a U-Turn Anyway?

*"If we are to go forward, we must go back and rediscover those precious values - that all reality hinges on moral foundations and that all reality has spiritual control."*

~ Martin Luther King, Jr. (1929-1968);
minister, civil rights activist

There are any number of reasons why we need to make a U-turn in our lives. Over the course of a lifetime each of us compiles so many experiences that, in the process, we can leave quite a few things undone, poorly done, or just plain overlooked and never addressed. For some of us, our conscience, or perhaps even an external event, will prod us to reconsider our actions. Consider this next story as a good example of this point.

A few years ago, I attended a family barbecue. Toward the end of the day, a group of about six or seven men were talking about our jobs, families and more. The beer was flowing and our tongues were loose. It was an unusual moment because the men were being very open about some of their very personal matters. There was a lot of complaining, and some of the stories sounded pretty serious.

After a while, the group broke up and I found myself alone with a twelve-year-old boy named Tom. Unbeknownst to us, he had been sitting for some time by himself, close enough to our group to hear all that was being said. Tom comes from a divorced family. His father left when he was very young and his mother remarried. From what I knew about the family, it did not seem like his new father cared very much for Tom. He looked at me and asked, "So Mr. R, if a person wanted to know the best way to live and make good decisions, is there a website or book he could go to in order to find out?"

I hadn't expected that kind of a question and I wasn't at all prepared to answer it. No one had ever asked me that before, and for that matter, I never thought about the question from the perspective of a young person. I responded with a question and asked him why he wanted to know. This was his answer: "Well, I was listening to all of those guys talking, and I don't want to screw my life up like they did."

Is that not an interesting observation? Tom was asking me for something that should be available to all of us, but especially to young folks. As I thought about it later, it seemed that he was asking for was a manual of "best practices" for living a successful life. And here I was at 58 years of age and unable to provide him with a good answer.

It is a very interesting question. How would you answer Tom? In the past, we would have directed him to a book like the Bible and then referred him to his parents for a more complete answer. But, as is the case with so many young people today, Tom is from a broken home. Divorce had taken its toll on him and others in his family. He probably felt that his mother and step-father were unable to give him good direction for one reason or another. As for the Bible, he would not even know how to begin to read it, let alone understand it.

This story can serve as the first reason why we need to make that U-turn. Our children are silently crying out for help in learning how to best live their lives. Older folks and educators alike believe that if we just provide the life skills information that young people need to know, they will pick it up over time and use it to their benefit.

As we can now see, merely providing life skills information may work for some but not for the vast majority of younger people. As we will discuss in the following chapters, I think we must not only teach them the best ways to live but we must then *show* them by our own example. This is easily said, but, considering how our culture works these days, it is very difficult to do.

Interestingly, the idea of older folks providing the information young people need to live better lives may have worked better for our generation when we were young because things were very different for us. Back in the 1950's and even '60's it seemed that there was more of a sense of real community. More people watched out and cared for not only their own children but also their neighbors'. We could rely on one another a lot more when out in public. Now it seems we must be on the lookout for those who are trying to hurt us and our children, rather than for those who might help us. As a consequence, people have learned to keep to themselves more and mind their own business. Today it seems folks are less likely to offer help and advice, especially to strangers. This pervasive type of isolation leaves young people more on their own today. In a sense, they have to rely on themselves to a greater degree than we did in a world that appears to be more hostile than the one we grew up in ourselves.

Again, I use the analogy of driving a car. A vehicle provides us with freedom of movement, the opportunity to get a job and much more. But if we abuse that privilege, accidents can occur and our lives may be permanently changed. Young drivers need

41

lessons and knowledge about the rules of the road, but they also need hands-on driving experience. When I was a teenager beginning to drive, I remember that my parents made me chauffeur them everywhere we went. They had me drive in neighborhoods, in parking lots, in the downtown business district and especially on the expressway. My father even took me out in a light winter storm to have me drive in the snow. They wanted me to be safe, so they gave me lots of driving experience. The same applies to our children and grandchildren with regard to life skills: if we want them to be safe in life and make good decisions, talk is not enough. We have to show them how.

As I sat in that AA meeting I mentioned earlier, I wondered what our generation might have done differently over the last 50 years. Could we have done more to help the young people at that meeting and others like them to avoid the addiction crisis in their lives? After all, it was on our generational watch when many things that were considered forbidden and "taboo" became legal, or at least much more acceptable. Take a look at the list of events that have occurred, for the most part, on our watch:

- In the early 1960's, public prayer in any active form is removed from our public educational system as well as our system of government.
- The divorce rate approaches the 50% level in the 1970's and remains there to this day. It has become a common and accepted practice for many in our general population and in some cases it is even considered inevitable.
- Abortion on demand becomes legal with Roe Vs. Wade in 1973, and since then (as of this writing), approximately 50 million babies have been terminated in the US alone.

- Over the last 50 years drug and alcohol usage, both legal and illegal, increases exponentially in the general population, especially among our youth.
- Bankruptcy becomes a common and accepted way to deal with unwanted debt. Personal filings for 2008 alone were just under one and a half million individuals. Each filing represents a family being negatively affected by the bankruptcy.
- Since the sexual revolution of the 1960's many treat sexual relations as a form of social recreation, especially our youth.
- Telling lies becomes even more of an accepted way of doing business on a commercial level. It has even become prevalent in how we deal with one another on a personal level. In politics especially, if it is possible, the level of dishonesty these days seems to have increased exponentially.
- The concept of personal responsibility is greatly diminished in importance in many roles of life.
- The pornography industry has grown to have larger revenues than Microsoft, Google, Amazon, eBay, Yahoo, Apple and Netflix combined. In 2006 worldwide pornography revenues ballooned to almost $100 billion.
- Abuse of food (obesity), money, sex, women, and most tragically, the molestation of children, become so commonplace that they are an expected part of our lives. Fewer and fewer people now seem to be outraged by any of these events when they occur.
- A growing number of families and children have to cope with absentee fathers. Statistics show that close to 40% of all children in the U.S. do not live with their biolog-

ical fathers. About 25% live with their single mothers.

- Illegitimate births which stood at 5% of all births in 1960 now stands in 2008 at an approximately 40% of all births

- Donations to church and charitable causes have remained at approximately 3% of our gross income (as it was in the year 1900) even during one of the greatest periods of financial growth in the late twentieth century.

- Our children are now blitzed with 24/7/365 availability of satellite TV feeds, MP3 players, iPods, laptop computers, smart phones, and the Internet. Of greatest concern is the surge in video gaming where the individual can compete electronically with literally anyone, anywhere, at any time in the world. And all of this communication takes place in isolation, unlike watching TV with the whole family as we did years ago. Much of this activity poses a direct challenge to faith and family core values and relatively few people are giving our youth any instruction as to how to properly balance these activities.

- With consideration to all of the above, it is no surprise that belief in God and matters of faith is largely viewed as being somewhat irrelevant by many young people. Consequently, many mainline churches have fewer and fewer young parishioners as members.

This disturbing list can go on even further. But if you look at each point individually, and then take them together as a whole, what can you conclude? What comes to mind for me are the following words of Jesus Christ. In Luke 17:1, He says:

*Things that cause people to sin are bound to come, but*
*woe to that person through whom they come.* (Luke 17:1)

For those of us who believe in God, these are chilling words.
Something major has changed on the Boomers' watch, and that
something has become a trend that is not good for any of us.
Do we bear any responsibility for these occurrences and their
consequences? After all, we were, and are, the people in charge.
Those younger than us look to us for guidance, direction and
permission to have the lifestyle they desire. Those older than us
seek respect from us. They want be sure that the children they
raised are living correctly and that they are guiding their own
children properly. There seems to be a great deal on our shoulders, a very great deal. Are we aware of that?

There may be those who read this and protest that he or she
personally had nothing to do with any of the negative developments described in the list above. They will say, "I did not have
a divorce or an abortion, nor was I responsible for taking prayer
out of the school system." That very well may be true. In fact, it
is true for most of us. But did we do anything to help prevent
or counteract those occurrences? Just as it was in the story of
the Good Samaritan, we may have not been the ones to beat
and rob that person on the road, but did we do anything to help
him? Or did we just look away and step over him as we came
upon him in the road?

There may also be those who say that they had to learn the
hard way as they grew up and so should young people today.
Life, they may say, is a great educator, and young people will
figure it out sooner or later. I agree with that sentiment, up to
a point. The process they speak of is something I call *"learning
by burning."* It can be a very expensive way to learn, and can fre-

quently leave unnecessary and permanent scars. Vernon Sanders Law once said,

> *Experience is a hard teacher because she gives the test first, the lesson afterwards.*

This kind of learning is ridiculously cruel. Its prevalence explains, in part at least, why things like the divorce rate still remains at close to 50%, even after all of these years. We older folks are not passing along the hard lessons learned from our experiences to our children. Younger people come along and fall prey to the same mistakes. Each and every person that has to reinvent the wheel goes through the same pain. The same could be said for many of our other social and financial issues.

The educational system in our country works hard at providing young folks with information so they can avoid many of life's pitfalls. But something seems to be missing from that system; something needs to be added. Passing the bulk of the responsibility for learning directly on to our children themselves may get us older folks off the hook, and we then can feel free from becoming personally involved in teaching young folks.

But can we honestly look at the list at the beginning of this chapter and feel that we have no responsibility at all for what has happened? Furthermore, should we feel no responsibility to help address the issues? I think we are looking at a second major reason for making a U-turn; these trends are not encouraging, and we must accept our responsibility to address them.

Let's carry this analysis to another level. It is sometimes said that there are only two things in life that are certain: death and taxes. Well, only half of that statement is now true. Many folks these days do not pay federal or state income taxes due to any number of reasons, legal or otherwise.

We are left with only one thing that for sure will happen to each of us: death. This brings us to the third and perhaps most compelling reason for making a U-turn. That reason is our mortality.

As I mentioned earlier, whenever a poll is taken which asks people about their belief in a life beyond our present one, a very high percentage claim to believe in such a life. Most of those people believe it will be a better life. If we honestly believe this is true, then wouldn't it make sense that there be some supernatural being responsible for creating and maintaining that new life? And wouldn't that mean there must be some gateway or crossover point from this life to the next one? If so, we could then logically theorize that the crossover event occurs when we die. Would we then encounter the supernatural creator of the afterlife? Who would that creator be?

Will it be Jesus, Allah, Buddha, Yahweh, or someone else? Should we choose to make no decision about this question in this life and just accept the final outcome, whatever it is? Can't we just leave it up to whoever presents himself at that moment? This subject comprises the most important question of our lives, and we need to answer it sooner rather than later.

The problem with the "whatever" option is that every major religion demands that its followers (1) believe in their god with all their heart, (2) adhere to the major precepts of their faith, and (3) profess their faith to others as part of the process of gaining their eternal life and reward. Therefore, it seems that we have to make a choice while we are alive, and it needs to be an actively managed choice that we live out each day. In all religions, once you make your choice openly, you are then expected to live in accordance with what you profess to believe. Your actions are taken as evidence and will serve as a form of confirmation of what you say you hold true.

In my case, my wife and I have done that for ourselves and our family. As it says in the book of Joshua:

> *But as for me and my household, we will serve the Lord.*
>
> (Joshua 24:15)

I cannot prove to you that I will be correct in my choice and that at the moment of our earthly death it will be Jesus who greets us at the crossover point. I can only tell you that I have given this a great deal of thought and have made Jesus Christ my choice. Logically, it then makes sense for me to live my life in such a way during the time I have remaining, so that when I meet Jesus, He will say:

> *Well done, good and faithful servant! You have been faithful with a few things; I will put you in charge of many things. Come and share your master's happiness!*
>
> (Matthew 25:21)

So let us assume for argument's sake that it will be Jesus. With regard to the current discussion at hand, what would please Him the most? What would make Him respond to us as in the Scripture above? Jesus did tell us something about teaching, training and caring for those around us. He made specific recommendations that we should follow with regard to our children and those younger than us. He did indeed make comments about this most important question concerning their salvation. Significantly, His last words to all of us are recorded in Matthew 28:19, where He said:

*Therefore go and make disciples of all nations, baptizing them in the name of the Father and of the Son and of the Holy Spirit, and teaching them to obey everything I have commanded you. And surely I am with you always, to the very end of the age.* (Matthew 28:19)

To make matters even more compelling, remember what He said earlier in the book of Matthew, specifically about children and those who are young in the faith.

*And whoever welcomes a little child like this in my name welcomes me. But if anyone causes one of these little ones who believe in me to sin, it would be better for him to have a large millstone hung around his neck and to be drowned in the depths of the sea. Woe to the world because of the things that cause people to sin! Such things must come, but woe to the man through whom they come.* (Matthew 18:6)

If you claim to believe in the Christian God and Trinity, then here is one of the most forceful reasons for making things right with those we may have hurt or failed to help in the past. If we truly consider ourselves Christians and followers of Jesus Christ, then His words must guide us.

To be clear on this point, true belief is not just consciously assenting to a concept. Certainly it does require mental agreement, but that agreement has to rise to such a level that we develop a passion for promoting the idea. With all of our passion for the concept, we grow to believe it so completely that we then incorporate it into our own personal daily actions. In other words, the passion becomes so great that it moves us to take action. That

49

is real belief. When Jesus used the word "belief" in all of His talks, that is exactly the kind of belief He meant. We must believe something so fervently that we live it out in our lives. The belief in Christ Himself and the inevitability of death therefore becomes the third, and most important, reason for us to make a U-turn.

But just in case you are still not convinced, I would like you to think about the following facts. In December 2006, the United Nations released a comprehensive report on world wealth. Here is the bottom line as to what was found. If you have $2,200 of wealth to your name, you are in the top 50% of the richest people in the world. If you have assets of at least $61,000 consisting of any kind of wealth, you are in the top 10% of the richest people. And finally, if you have $500,000 or more of wealth to your name, you are in the top 1% of the world's richest people. Out of more than six billion people in the world, there are roughly 37 million people in this topmost category and many of those reading this fall into that group. Therefore, by this rating system, many of us are considered very rich when compared to the rest of the world. I have to believe that this is how God sees it as well.

I never thought I would be in the category of the world's richest people financially. When I first read this, what came to mind was the following passage, spoken by Jesus Himself:

> **From everyone who has been given much, much will be demanded; and from the one who has been entrusted with much, much more will be asked.** (Luke 12:48)

If we are truly the richest people in the world according to these U.N. statistics, then what will God expect us to do with our wealth? Remember, in God's eyes wealth consists not only of physical wealth but also all of the other talents and special gifts we possess. We must also consider whether the wealth is really ours or His. The verse above suggests that He is expecting us to put *His* money and the other talents He gives us to such use as to benefit the neediest in the world. But before we go off to the world's poorest countries to help, we need to ask ourselves who in our immediate world needs our help? You may not have to look very far for someone to help with your money and resources.

Another way to express the Luke 12 passage would be "To whom much has been given, much will be required." That is serious food for thought. Why do we need to make a U-turn? Because God has blessed us beyond all reasonable expectations and He expects us to use those gifts to bless others.

Here are some additional reasons: it was on our generational watch when prayer was taken out of our schools; our generation has largely stopped attending mainline religious services; and we have worked very hard at removing our Christian faith from the educational system, state and local governments, the marketplace, and public view. We can now see the results of this intentional drift away from God.

As a result, study after study tell us that many in the millennial generation (those born between 1982 and 2000) find organized religion and faith a waste of time and irrelevant for solving many current issues. Don't we share some of the blame for the development of that opinion in our children? Have our actions or inactions helped our families and country grow in the right direction? Do we at least owe our children an explanation, if not an apology and corrective action for our poor spiritual leadership?

Ask yourself this: if you are a Christian who believes in Jesus Christ, what do you believe is His greatest concern? I believe His mission was plain for all to see. He said:

*For the Son of man came to seek and save that which
was lost.*                                        (Luke 19:10)

Jesus' name literally means "Savior" and clearly indicates His
purpose. If saving people was His chief concern, then what should
be our major focus? Should we not be concerned with the same
thing? Remember, the definition of a true Christian is someone
who is an active follower of Jesus Christ and who professes His
teachings to others and who believes in them so much that he or
she applies them in daily life. What do you think He will say to
us when we meet Him as we cross over into the next life? We will
of course want to enter that life. But wouldn't it be logical for
Him to use that next life as an incentive now and a reward later
for those that did as He instructed? (See Matthew 25:31-46.)

From a spiritual perspective, have we been leading our children and subsequent generations in a direction toward God? Or
have we been leading them away from Him? The list of statistics
presented earlier can only be interpreted one way. If we are at
all concerned about God, matters of faith and our own salvation,
then this question is the one we need to deal with urgently as
we consider whether or not we should make a U-turn.

Young people want to know how to live correctly. They do
not want to make the same mistakes that their elders have made.
Many have seen and personally experienced the results of
divorce, bankruptcy, unwanted pregnancy, and drug and alcohol
abuse. They want to avoid all that if at all possible. Can you
blame them? But they hear no clear message from any credible
older person these days about what path to take. There simply
are too few heroes or role models to follow. We seem to say to
them that every religion is okay to follow, all choices are pretty
much equal in value and whatever path they choose to take in

life will get them to where they want to be eventually. In addition, we seem to say to them that some paths may take longer to travel but there are really no differences. We go even further by setting an example for them that says that if you do not want to go to church, that's okay too. It's up to you!

The concept of best practices seems to be a foreign one in the raising of our children. We seem to be putting all of the available life choices on a menu and just letting them choose for themselves. And then we do everything we can to prevent them from experiencing failure. We intervene at every level and opportunity. The young folks learn to live life as if they will always have a safety net beneath them. That is not how the world works though; rules and laws govern every part of our lives. Of course we all know that there are ways around many of these laws, chief of which is non-compliance. How do the young folks come to learn this? They simply have to watch our actions and watch the news. Our behavior says it all. We have done them a great disservice.

Our generation has never wanted, and still does not want, to commit ourselves by picking only one set of rules to live by. After all, we don't want to seem narrow minded or exclusive. If we believe this to be the case, and we argue that this is the right way to live, then how can we possibly look at the statistics I listed earlier and say that we have been successful?

What did Jesus do? He certainly picked one set of laws to follow. He taught people to live a definite way. If anyone had an "exclusive" way to live, He certainly did. So, was He being narrow minded? Was He wrong? No, He simply was telling and showing everyone, *from an eternal perspective,* the best practices for successful living.

The Sermon on the Mount is filled with practical advice for good ways to live. I love the book of Proverbs as well. As you read through the verses you realize that even thousands of years ago people knew the best ways to live. So what happened? How did we become so ignorant in the two to three thousand years since then? We will address this question in a future chapter.

One significant problem we have these days is that our generation has mainly focused on the fight between the Right and the Left of the political spectrum. Instead of right versus left, we should be telling young folks about right versus wrong. More importantly, we should be *showing* them the difference between right and wrong in the way we live our lives. Growing up, most of us young folks knew the difference between right and wrong, and we knew that if we did something wrong and got caught, we would pay for it. Many times we still did what was wrong but when we got caught we accepted the punishment; we knew the law and knew the consequences for breaking it. Can we honestly say that about most young people today? For that matter, can we even say that about us as older folks?

Generally speaking, many of today's youth do not seem to know the difference between right and wrong. As a consequence they are learning about life more from what is "caught rather than what is taught." They watch us and see how we are living and follow our lead. They have received the message; they have caught the lesson. Can we honestly say that this system is working to anyone's advantage? Like it or not, we are their teachers. As of this writing I have a two-year-old grandson. I am constantly amazed at what he knows and what he can do even at such a tender young age. He watches everything we do and he learns. He catches most everything he sees and hears.

So, where does this leave us? Many in our generation say that we believe in the God of the Bible and in the end we would like to gain entrance into Heaven. We want to think that, for the most part, we are good people and have followed the core precepts of our Christian faith. But, in fact, is all of this true? If our biggest concern in life is making sure that we are in close connection with God and doing His will, then have we been doing that to the level He expects? If not, then this fact alone is enough of a reason for making a U-turn. Go back over the gospels for yourself. Read the words of Christ and see if you have been in compliance with His expectations or not.

Some reading this may scoff at these proposals. If you do not believe in a God that created our entire world and that He is the one who rules it according to a given set of laws, then it would seem you have little to be concerned about. Your life plan should be to simply eat, drink, and be merry. Just make sure you do not run afoul of the IRS, state police, or any of our earthly laws.

But consider these questions. If there is a Creator who made the cosmos, and who maintains the earth and all of its life, including the life after this one, then would He not give us His laws to live by? Can we see laws in place that govern and regulate all of nature? Of course we can. Every morning the sun rises, the earth keeps turning with exact precision and in most cases our bodies keep going, despite how we treat them sometimes.

We witness the universe and these marvelous examples proving that God does exist and of how God works. Certainly no human being has put all of this together, so isn't it sensible for us to believe that God's words in Scripture are true? If He put into place a series of complicated laws to govern all of nature, then surely He created us with a similar set of laws and rules. Why would He make us, His greatest creation, and not give us a book of instructions or an "operator's manual" to follow?

Finally I offer one more interesting reason for making a U-turn. In the Christian faith there exists a popular concept which has become commonly known as "developing a close personal relationship with Jesus Christ." The idea is to manage your life and daily tasks with a sense of prayerful reliance on God. Many people go about their business each day asking God for His help and thanking Him when the occasion arises. It is an interesting way to live. But when we think about this concept objectively, it does make a great deal of sense. If we claim to believe in God and all the truths we find in the Bible, then we would be foolish, to the point of being suicidal, if we did not rely on an active relationship with our Creator. After all, we understand Him as a being who has perfect knowledge and knows what is best for us.

In the process of experiencing this kind of relationship, we will receive from Him by way of His Holy Spirit a sense of what is best for us and what we should avoid. He will also provide us with wisdom about our future plans and hopes. He will give us our best practices. Since He has such a clear view of our future, it is logical that He will be dropping hints to us. If we are listening closely enough, we can gain insight into our future. These are very valuable thoughts and should be recorded or written in a place that we can easily refer to in the future. Here is another good reason for a U-turn. At the time we feel we have received a revelation from God, we are likely to be excited. But after a while, the excitement recedes and we are off to do other things.

Try to keep track of special moments when you feel that God has spoken to you. The messages He sends may appear simple on the surface but can often contain other deeply embedded thoughts and instruction, especially for the distant future. But many of us move at a fast pace and can easily forget the messages received while having a mountain-top experience. Go back and find those messages. Rediscover what God was saying to you at that moment. It very often will have an impact on your future.

It is true; we may have to go back in order to move forward.

There are many other reasons for making a U-turn; the list is endless. But quite frankly, to my way of thinking, the above reasons are the best ones. As you read this, your conscience may be shouting out to you. You know there may be things from your past, as well as from the present, that should be corrected or changed. At least the effort should be made to try and repair those things and resolve issues if possible. Do your best with the resources you have to make it right and then leave the rest up to God.

The bottom line is that you know in your heart that you will be seeing God on that last day. Why take a chance and ignore this opportunity to use the rest of your life to make certain that you are making God happy? Remember what is at stake here: eternity. That means forever. It is impossible to understand that concept of eternity completely because we have nothing in our human experience that lasts forever. Contemplation of eternity alone should be enough to move us forward and begin making the U-turn.

Now that we have some idea as to why we need to make a U-turn, let's talk about why we do *not* need to make one. Let me play the devil's advocate. I think you will find this interesting.

*"Be kind, for everyone you meet is fighting a hard battle."*
~ Plato (427-347);
Classical Greek philosopher

# 4

## Some Reasons Why We Do *Not* Need to Make a U-Turn

*"Reflect upon your blessings, of which every man has plenty, not on your past misfortunes, of which all men have some."*

~ Charles Dickens (1812-1870);
novelist

It was one of those odd and uncomfortable conversations you have with a person while having a few drinks at the end of the day. I had known Jake for quite some time but never really sat down and had any kind of a heart-to-heart talk with him. Jake, who was 66 years old at the time, was raised a Catholic but, somewhere along the line, had stopped going to church and stopped believing that God was really concerned about him personally. Matters of faith became something he rarely thought about.

We were sitting in a quiet corner of a bar when he began to tell me about his 95-year-old father's dilemma. He described the situation this way:

*...Yeah, my father just keeps going. He's 95 years old now and just won't give up the ghost. You know, I've been waiting for him to finally let go for a long time now. After all, his life can't be much fun. For the last 10 years or so*

*he's been taking a pile of pills every day and he can't really
get around. He's had his run. And it isn't very fair to me.
I've been the one who has to look after him and deal with
the nursing home and insurance issues. My brother doesn't
lift a finger to help, and never has. But I know my father
fights the thought of leaving. He's as much as told me so.
And I don't know what he's afraid of. After all, he is going
to a better place.*

What was so interesting about this discussion was that Jake admitted to me that he really did not believe in God or, more accurately, that he was very skeptical about the reality of a supernatural creator. But here he was stating beyond a doubt that he believed that the life after this one would be a better place. How could that make sense? If there is no God or supernatural entity, then who or what would have created the next life? Who would maintain it and be responsible for it? I believe that Jake is not alone in his expectations.

You often hear the same kind of comment at a funeral. We sometimes attempt to console the bereaved by stating that the deceased is in a better place. Some of us will go so far as to say that they are certain the person is in Heaven as they speak. It is a comforting thought, I will admit that. But this expectation gets at the core of the point I want to make about not having to make a U-turn.

Throughout our lives as Baby Boomers, many of us have gotten whatever we wanted. And so we reason, why should it be any different in death? Why shouldn't there be a place like Heaven waiting for us on the other side? We might apply that same line of reasoning to the question before us: why bother with the U-turn and any attempt at restoring old relationships if, in the end, we all get to go to Heaven anyway? It's a good question, since I believe that many, many people secretly think this way.

There are numerous variations on people's expectations regarding admission into Heaven. There are Christians who believe if you have accepted Christ into your life, that's it, you are saved no matter what happens afterward. There are others who say that when Jesus died on the cross, His death "automatically" guaranteed entrance for all into Heaven. There are those who don't know what to think and shrug off the question. These folks are willing to accept the default position; whatever or whoever shows up on the other side—Jesus, Allah, Buddha— is okay with them.

Basically, the expectation is that whatever is coming simply has to be better than this life. What scares me most about this conversation is how cavalier so many of us are about our eternal futures. We are betting everything we have and will have, including our souls, on an "iffy" proposition.

Remember, we are going to be dead a lot longer than we were alive. As a matter of fact, there is no comparison. How do you compare an average 85-year existence with the concept of living forever? I think people rely on the fact that God is good and in the end He will relent and let us all into Heaven. People just do not believe that He could be so harsh as to send anyone into everlasting fire and pain. Therefore, we conclude that making a U-turn is a waste of time. Personally, I would like to agree with that opinion, but there is one thing that prevents me from doing so, and that is the Scriptures.

There simply is no evidence anywhere in the Bible that God will admit everyone to Heaven and eternal life in the end. As a matter of fact there is ample evidence that the opposite will happen. Since this is such an important point, and because it can be a major reason for feeling it's unnecessary to go through the effort of making a U-turn, I would like to spend some time presenting a few other related observations.

When was the last time you were in serious trouble? Have you ever been in a situation where you thought you might actually die? Or maybe you're like me and you've never experienced anything so frightening or serious. I suspect that most of us fall into this second category.

I wonder though. When you watch the television news every day and listen to friends and relatives talk, you can easily get the impression that there are many things that can hurt you in the world. Hearing about these things may scare us from time to time, and even though they may seem widespread, few of us expect to personally experience such things. Many of us feel that medical and money problems, work-related issues and even more serious concerns can usually be successfully dealt with in some way. If we cannot deal with them successfully, and we find ourselves faced with the prospect of death, so be it. After all, we'll be going to a better place. Isn't that true? When we lose a loved one, the standard words of consolation seem to be "I'm sorry for your loss; I'm sure that he (or she) is in a better place." How do we know that is true?

Jesus gives us a very different story:

> *Do not be afraid of those who kill the body but cannot kill the soul. Rather, be afraid of the One who can destroy both soul and body in hell.* (Matthew 10:28)

According to Jesus, it seems that there is another level of threat to us, not only in this life but, more importantly, in the next. That threat is greater because there is no relief or parole from the place we call Hell. Is it possible that we are at serious risk for our eternal lives but not really know it? Is it possible that many of us will not be going to Heaven after all?

The truth is that many people expect to automatically go to Heaven after they die. As I said earlier, poll after poll indicate that the vast majority of us believe in a life after this one and that we will go to Heaven when we pass from this life. The idea of going to a place like Hell is just so unthinkable that we don't even consider it a possibility, and the average person usually dismisses it outright. But if we look closely and objectively at the main construct of all Christianity, the death of Jesus Christ, we might start to think differently about the possibilities concerning our eternal destiny.

The unfounded assumption that we will be granted eternal life is a major reason why people feel we do not have to worry about our salvation, and that everything will be okay in the end without having to make a U-turn. I would like to offer some reasons why this thinking is seriously flawed. What follows are a few logical and common-sense observations about the crucifixion of Christ, an event that many of us today have come to take for granted. The cross of Christ gives us many clues as to how we might be spending our eternal lives.

## Clue #1:

All Christians believe (or should believe) that Jesus died for our sins on the cross. We also believe that He rose from the dead and ascended into Heaven. The cross is at the heart and center of all Christianity. Without it Christianity loses all of its substance and meaning. Since we believe this is true, then we also must believe that God Himself allowed the cross to occur.

In fact, Scripture tells us that God approved of the plan to redeem mankind.

> *Yet it was the LORD's will to crush him and cause him to suffer, and though the LORD makes his life a guilt offering, he will see his offspring and prolong his days, and the will of the LORD will prosper in his hand.*
>
> (Isaiah 53:10)

But think about it. The plan was to have His only Son, a supreme being like Himself, yield Himself to people like us and be tortured and crucified to death in order to atone for our sins. This was the plan God Himself designed and executed.

How can we begin to assign a cost to such an act? What would make Him agree to such a plan? What else is going on around us now that would seem to dictate the need for such a drastic action? We are told that our sins caused a break in the relationship we had with God. To re-establish that connection, a savior or redeemer had to be sacrificed. Couldn't God have found an easier way to solve the problem of sin in the world? Or could it instead be that we have not taken the time to understand how God and His laws work?

Is it possible that God cannot just do whatever He pleases at any time because He Himself is subject to who He is and how He must act? In other words, maybe God is a certain way. Maybe He exists as a being with very specific characteristics, and His thoughts and actions are subject to His own specific nature? Just as all of nature is subject to physical laws, might God also be subject to His own set of supernatural and spiritual laws? When it comes time to deal with each of us, will He judge us according to His specific nature as reflected in the Scriptures?

**Clue #2:**

They call Jesus "the Savior." Why? What did He save us from? The standard answer provided by Christian doctrine is that He saved us from our sins. But why? What are our sins going to do to us? Could the damage they inflict on us be so great as to warrant the death of a supreme being? Again the standard answer is that He died to save us from eternal damnation, or what we commonly refer to as Hell. But as the polls show, most people don't think they'll be going to Hell. Many for that matter, do not even believe such a place exists.

We need to ask if there is really a place called Hell that threatens all of us or not. The fact that God thought we needed a Savior to save us from something so horrifying, and that He was willing to give up His Son to such a horrible death should stop us dead in our tracks. There has to be something we do not understand that threatens us on an earthly and eternal level. It seems that something else must be going on around us now and that we cannot fully appreciate its potential to hurt us. It must be huge beyond all comprehension. It is threatening us now in this life, in our eternal future, and many of us are not even taking the time to try and understand it. The fact that God allowed His Son to die in the way He did is an indication that we are indeed living at great risk as human beings.

**Clue #3:**

The cross of Christ proves that there must be a Hell, and that the threat to us is very real, very severe and absolutely permanent. For if this was not true, we wouldn't need a Savior. Similarly, this holds true for those who believe there is a Hell but that we will all be forgiven on that last day and go to Heaven. Aside from the fact that this thinking contradicts all of Scripture (see Matthew 25:31-40), it makes no sense. If God, who is all-knowing, knew that the threat to us would be removed by His pardoning everyone in the end, then His Son did not have to suffer such torture and death. In fact, if there is no Hell, then we wouldn't need the Scriptures either. The Bible itself becomes totally unnecessary, as do all of the churches, clergy, doctrine, saints and martyrs over the ages.

### Clue #4:

The cross proves there must only be one way into Heaven. Again, if we could achieve eternal life through another set of beliefs or religion, then Jesus would not have had to die. His death would be meaningless. We could get to Heaven by other means or through less-demanding faith systems. No other world religion claims to follow a god or leader that died for his or her followers so they might gain the benefits of eternal life. But I will state here that I fully expect to see people of other faiths in Heaven on that last day. How God will work that out I do not know. Does this, in turn, mean that we can choose any religion to follow? Not for me. I have met Jesus personally and I am convinced He is the truth, the way and the life.

### Clue #5:

The cross proves that there must be an afterlife. Again, there would be no need for Christ to die for us otherwise. If after we die there is in fact no conscious existence in a new life, then the life we have now is all there is. If this is the case, then we should all just eat, drink, and be merry since there is nothing but the grave beyond this life. But this obviously is not the message of the Bible. If we are to believe that this mortal life is all there is, then all of Scripture must be denied along with all of the sacrifices made by millions of Christians since the time of Christ. Could they all be wrong?

**Clue #6:**

The cross of Christ proves that this was the best solution that God Himself could devise to solve the problem of sin. This fact cannot be overstated. God answers to no one. Even so, He chose to save us in such a way that would ultimately cost God the Father, God the Son and God the Holy Spirit more than any of us could ever begin to understand. One might think that, after God saw how man would repeatedly disappoint Him by choosing to sin, He would have just given up on us. But instead He continually extends Himself and reaches out to us through His Son. Why would there only be one way out of the problem posed by sin? Why would God agree to take such a drastic action? As I argued earlier, it would seem that there must be a simpler solution. The Bible tells us that,

> *God loved the world so much that He gave His only Son, so that anyone who believes in Him shall not perish but have eternal life.* (John 3:16)

What explains the length to which God will go to offer us salvation? Is it possible that God loves us in such a way that He actually, in a sense, "needs" our love? After all, when we fall in love with another person it is very common to feel a strong need for their personal love and attention. Since the Scriptures tell us that we are all made in God's likeness, is it possible that He too has a similar kind of personal need for our love? This would help explain why God felt He had to sacrifice His Son to save us. Another fact to consider is that God knew that man was destined to choose sin, and that He would have to send His Son to earth to repair the relationship. Even with that knowledge, God chose to move forward with the plan of creation. In a way, we do the same thing when we choose to marry someone. We tend to overlook their faults in order to gain their love. We know their love will cost us, but in the long run, it will be worth that cost. In this sense, we make the same choice when we get married that God made when He created us.

## Clue #7:

The cross proves that our free will can literally "trump" God's will. We always have a choice to make. Every day, we must choose between the way of the world or the way of the cross. Even in the Garden of Eden, before Adam and Eve disobeyed God and the Garden was still a perfect paradise, there was the presence of the snake. Did you ever wonder where the snake came from? Obviously God allowed it into the Garden, and through the temptation offered by the snake, Adam and Eve chose to disappoint God with their sin. They used their trump card to follow their own desires. The results were devastating to them and to all of mankind.

They chose their own will over God's will. Therefore God reacted and He honored their choice allowing them to have their sin and its consequences. Some people will scoff at the story of Adam and Eve as being silly and no more than a fairy tale, and that is fine. Even without Adam and Eve to condemn us, we have committed enough sins of our own over the ages to put us in a bad place with respect to God. Adam and Eve ate one or two of the banned apples, while we, in the centuries since, have gone ahead and planted whole vineyards of "forbidden fruit" and eat from them at will! Who is in more trouble?

Remember also that God will never force anyone to go to Heaven. He will allow us to have our free will and the consequences of our choices. Even as He was dying on the cross, each of the two thieves who were crucified with Him made their own choice. One chose Christ and the other did not. The cross did not automatically open the gates of Heaven to both men. Only those who want to go to Heaven will go there. There is always a choice and the choice is ours.

### Clue #8:

The cross of Christ is usually thought of from our own temporal point of view. We learn that Christ saved us from our sins. But what did the cross do to the relationship of the Trinity? When Moses went up the mountain to meet with God and he asked God His name, God told him that His name was "I am" (see Exodus 3:14). In other words, the Trinity of God the Father, Son and Holy Spirit just *is* as it *is,* and so the relationship of the Father to the Son also *is.* The Trinity has no beginning, middle or end in time. Time only exists as an earthly concept for us and all that is in the physical universe.

God created the universe and all that is in it, including man. But the universe is subject to what is known as time and space. In other words, everything is temporary and, in time, it will pass away. However, God allowed the event of the cross, something that happened in the temporal world, to affect all of eternity. It altered, even for a short while, the relationship between God the Father and His Son. Once again, we have no way to appreciate the meaning and importance of this fact. But we can stand in awe of this occurrence and realize that God would never have allowed anything like that to change the sacred relationship with His Son *unless* there was something so incomprehensively huge at stake that threatened everything that is important to God, including our eternal lives.

**Clue #9:**

The cross reveals to us another important fact. Before Jesus went to the cross, He spent time in the Garden of Gethsemane agonizing over what was to come. It has always bothered me that it appeared Jesus was afraid to die on the cross. We find Him sweating great drops of blood and asking God to relieve Him of the task before Him (Luke 22:41-44). Even though He was human and His agony is easily understood from a human perspective, He was also divine, and one would think that He was bestowed with the physical fortitude and strength to endure His fate without looking for a way out. It appears that there must be more to it.

As I explained earlier, I think the answer to the question surrounding Christ's agony was that it was not as much caused by the anticipated physical pain and suffering as it was about His being separated from His Father. When Jesus took on all of our sins upon Himself on the cross, God had to turn from Him. God cannot look upon sin. He cannot coexist in the presence of sin. That is why Jesus cried out on the cross, "My God, my God, why have you forsaken me?"

The sin Christ took on Himself altered, for a while, the eternal closeness He always knew with God and Jesus had never experienced this separation before. The temporal was allowed to affect the eternal. That is just simply incredible. This was the principal reason why Jesus was in agony in the Garden. He knew this was about to occur and He could barely endure the thought, even though the separation would only be for a short while.

What then does all this mean for us? If Hell is the state of being eternally separated from God, and Jesus Himself was in such a state of distress over being separated from God for just a few hours or days, how then should we view the prospect of Hell? Can we be so sure that Hell is not real or is at least something that is not meant for us? Can it be possible that some of us think that even if we end up in Hell, it will not be so bad? We are gambling with our eternal lives.

We need, then, to ask ourselves: are we in trouble or not? Can we look on the cross of Christ as something that happened between God and Jesus and maybe just concerns us a little, at most? Or is there now a sense that something very serious is going on around you and that it directly concerns you and me? Do you think that God is trying to save us through His Son or not? Would you agree that the sacrifice that Jesus made for us is profound beyond all measure and requires a commensurate response from us?

If so, then the question about whether or not we need to make a U-turn in this life becomes incredibly important. Your answer can have eternal consequences for you and perhaps many others in your life.

Your next step is either to ignore what you've just read or to pursue an answer to these questions. Unfortunately, the urge to ignore these thoughts will be strong since, as we know, many do not think that entrance into Heaven will be denied them. This thought is so repugnant and frightening that it causes many to refuse to investigate the possibility it is true. This stems from a core characteristic of our American culture to expect to receive all that we want and need; if you think about it, never before in history have so many people received so much of what they want as they have over the last 50 or 60 years. It makes sense, therefore, that many think this will translate to their personal salvation, and they do not feel the need to go back to their past transgressions and make things right. They assume that salvation is their *right*, regardless of their worthiness and compliance with God's laws.

However, if you want to know more about these questions, you need to personally meet Christ in the Gospels. Find a well-translated Bible with footnotes and commentary that help explain the words of Christ. The Holy Spirit will tutor you as you seek Him and the answers you need. Don't give up, there's too much at stake for you and those around you. What you do now will affect the rest of your life and possibly the lives of those closest to you in both this world and the next.

In addition to the unreasonable expectation of guaranteed salvation, there are other reasons why people might feel that making a U-turn is unnecessary. I will list some I have heard from individuals:

- It's too much work and I just do not have the stomach to go back and open up that "can of worms" with my father and other relatives.
- I would like to go back and make it right but they'll never listen to me. I haven't talked to my brother in over 20 years. I know he hates me.
- I just do not have the time right now to begin a process like that. It will take many hours, perhaps days to put the old issues "to bed" and be done with them. Besides I don't even remember all of the details.
- It's too late now. My mother died five years ago.
- I am so embarrassed over what I did back then. I just cannot face those people ever again.

- It was not my fault! If anything it was my actions that prevented something tragic from happening, but they all blamed me. I will never forgive them for what they said and did to me!
- I lost so much money because of my sister or that business partner I had. I could have sued her/him and probably should have just to prove my point.
- It was my husband's fault. His stubbornness prevented us from reconciling with my family. There is nothing I can do now. He is gone now forever.

I could go on with many more examples. It seems I've heard all of the reasons why a U-turn is not possible. But I would answer all of the people who feel this way with one comment. Suppose there is a Hell after this life and suppose our sins do condemn us to that place but for the grace of God. And what if the people that have hurt you or whom you have hurt still have an open wound and are suffering because of what happened between you? If that wound has been festering all this time, contributing to their bitterness and preventing them from accepting Christ into their lives, will you be able to live with the thought that this could keep them, and others around them, from reaching Heaven in the end? Are you willing to accept that responsibility? Are you certain that God sees the excuses listed above in the same light as you see them?

Hatred and holding a grudge have the ability to poison a person's whole being. It rots the soul from the inside out, much like a spiritual acid. As a consequence the person in question becomes blind to the effect that poison is having on their attitude and their relationship with others. It takes all the love out of us and replaces it with the opposite of love — hatred and apathy. Even if you were not directly at fault in causing pain to others, can you be the one to bring healing to them? What would Jesus do? What did He do in situations like these? What did He advocate?

We can come up with many reasons for not having to make a U-turn. But I can tell you that I have yet to hear one that makes any sense. Do whatever you have to do to make it right whether it's your fault or not. I will close this chapter with the beautiful words of Jesus as He gives us the Beatitudes. Read them closely; this is how Jesus advised us to live. These are the ultimate best practices for successful living.

*Now when he saw the crowds, he went up on a mountainside and sat down. His disciples came to him, and he began to teach them, saying:*
*"Blessed are the poor in spirit, for theirs is the kingdom of heaven.*
*Blessed are those who mourn, for they will be comforted.*
*Blessed are the meek, for they will inherit the earth.*
*Blessed are those who hunger and thirst for righteousness, for they will be filled.*
*Blessed are the merciful, for they will be shown mercy.*
*Blessed are the pure in heart, for they will see God.*
*Blessed are the peacemakers, for they will be called sons of God.*
*Blessed are those who are persecuted because of righteousness, for theirs is the kingdom of heaven.*

*Blessed are you when people insult you, persecute you and falsely say all kinds of evil against you because of me. Rejoice and be glad, because great is your reward in heaven, for in the same way they persecuted the prophets who were before you."* (Matthew 5:1-12)

*"Always hold your head up, but be careful to keep your nose at a friendly level."*

~ Max L. Forman (1909-90);
Jewish-American writer

# 5
## What's So Difficult About Making a U-Turn?

*"Don't wait until everything is just right. It will never be perfect. There will always be challenges, obstacles and less than perfect conditions. So what. Get started now. With each step you take, you will grow stronger and stronger, more and more skilled, more and more self-confident and more and more successful."*

~ Mark Victor Hansen;
author, speaker

My wife and I, along with another couple, were on our way to a party but we got a late start and it looked like we were going to be a little late. I hate being late for anything. As we pulled out of our driveway, my wife asked me if I knew where we were going and I impatiently answered her, "Yes, yes, don't worry." We were headed to an area of our state that I rarely travel to, but I felt confident we would find the house. However, it turned out that my confidence was misguided. We got lost, I had to make many U-turns, and yes, I even had to stop and ask for directions. Eventually we found the place but at that point we were very late and I was very embarrassed.

I learned an important lesson that evening about being pre-pared. As I look back on that experience I realize that much more was going on as we tried to find the correct way to the party. Making my first of many U-turns that evening was a tacit admission that I had made a mistake. People in the car started to wonder if I really knew how to get there. When I was forced to make a second U-turn, I had to admit that I was lost and it became obvious that I definitely did not know where we were going. Not only were we late but I was the reason everyone else was late as well.

Here are some of the thoughts I had about what was really going on that evening as I was making all of those avoidable U-turns:

- I had to admit to everyone in the car that I was wrong and I did not know where I was going. I allowed myself to get caught in an avoidable problem; I should have known better and I should have prepared better.
- Turning around seemed to waste more time because I was now heading back over ground that I already covered. And every time I made another U-turn, it made me feel even worse and more frustrated.
- Even though it became obvious that we were on the wrong road, I felt like we would eventually find our way and it would all work out okay. So I was reluctant to turn back. My pride forced me to continue our forward movement.
- I was seething with anger at myself for not preparing better and getting the right directions.
- I have always been very good with directions and I pride myself on being the "driver" in the family who always knew where he was going and who could get us to our destination on time.

- I had lost control of the situation and I was no longer in charge. Others in the car wanted to help correct our problem. I felt I had to save face and reassert my leadership role even though it was obvious I was not in control of the situation.
- I was embarrassed, and the one thing I was always good at doing was now turning out poorly, and people would question my abilities in this area in the future. So there would be future consequences as well.
- When we arrived at the party I had to find a way to make an excuse for being late that didn't sound like I was lost, but that also sounded truthful to the others in the car with me.
- What was to be a fun time turned into a stressful time, and that fact upset me even more.
- I had to endure the greatest humiliation of all. I had to stop and ask someone for directions.
- On top of all of this, when on past trips someone in the car would suggest that we might have to make a U-turn, I would always reply, "I don't do U-turns." And here I had to make one U-turn after another and we were still lost.
- But in the end I was greatly relieved to arrive at the party and had to admit that the U-turns did eventually help us find our way.

So why is this story so important? I believe it reveals a great deal about why many of us Baby Boomers find ourselves in near bankrupt condition in so many areas of our lives. Whether it concerns finances, politics, matters of faith, family relationships, work-related issues, or recreational endeavors and temptations that beset us every day, we often choose the incorrect way of dealing with these challenges.

Instead of admitting that we might have the wrong idea or an insufficient plan when things start to go wrong, and then taking the steps to check whether we are on the right track, we continue to push forward on our current course, all the while knowing that we are probably on the wrong road. As a consequence we oftentimes find ourselves "lost in the wilderness" with our problems, and with no easy way of fixing them.

Many of us agree that something has to change in the way we live these days. However, we want the kind of change that will get us back on the right track as long as we ourselves do not have to change very much of our daily routines. And we don't want it to cost much to do it.

If we continue to use the illustration of driving a car as an analogy for how we live our lives, then as I said earlier, there are four choices before us. As we approach a major crossroad, we could turn left, turn right, continue on the same road or go back. The first three are relatively easy to do compared to the last option. As many of us know, people generally develop a set of beliefs over the course of their lives. Our words and actions reflect these beliefs. Some of us actually become identified by, and with, our beliefs.

Once we stake out a certain "belief territory" for ourselves it can be very hard for us to change our way of life by admitting we were wrong. Our pride may not allow us to do so. This is not unlike my driving story; my pride got in the way of finding a good solution more quickly. And so it is with many of us.

But today, with all of the challenging issues we face, we may sense the need to make some change in our heading. We always seem to try to find a solution to our problems that fits into our current set of values and beliefs, thereby allowing us to hold onto most of our old way of thinking. We are very reluctant to make dramatic changes that take us out of our comfort zone.

We instead find a way to solve a problem by moving deeper into our old comfortable way of thinking. The fact that we at least made some kind of change is a comforting one to us and helps us feel as if we are making the necessary adjustments. It's as if we decided to get off the back road and take the super highway. It is a change, but we may still be headed in the wrong direction.

The truth is that, as always, we addressed the problem with the tools we were familiar with and that were at our disposal at the time. If we cannot admit as much, then we will probably fail in dealing successfully with the issues that will confront us in the future. We may be very comfortable in using a hammer in our work but that is usually not what is needed to fix a leaky faucet. Sometimes it takes a new set of tools and a new way of thinking to meet a challenge successfully.

All of this tends to move us deeper and further along into an extreme position, since we refuse to abandon our old way of thinking. Our stubbornness moves us further from a good solution. The problem with taking an extreme position is that it is narrow and unyielding and leaves no maneuvering room for making a change like a proper U-turn. We can find that we've "painted ourselves into a corner," so to speak.

But we must be careful here. Some of the "older ways of thinking" may be core values that are precious and that need to be preserved. They must be identified as such. They should become part of our best practices and be kept. But the ability to discern the difference between a valuable core principle and a way of thinking that is simply politically correct or fashionable at the time is also important to preserve. A good way to determine if a certain concept or older way of thinking is valuable or not is to look for evidence as to its effectiveness for those who lived in past generations. For example, when your grandfather advised you that "a penny saved is a penny earned," did you think it was a concept you should live your life by? Did it work for people in his day? Is it therefore worth keeping as a key truth?

When considering all of our options in solving a problem, we cannot assume that the original heading, beliefs and choices we've made thus far have been basically correct. And we cannot assume that all we need to do is to tweak or modify slightly our thinking toward any newly developing issues or future decisions.

What if we are on the wrong road to begin with? And, even worse, what if we have been on that road for a long time and have been moving directly away from the correct destination? What should we do now? If all of those who depend on us for guidance and support have been following us, they too could be very far from their proper destination. We need to take corrective action yesterday!

To many, it is unthinkable that we could be so wrong-headed in an age where it seems that we have accomplished so much. Our technological advances alone give us the impression that we have made great progress, not only in this one area of our lives, but in most other areas of our lives as well. However, this is not necessarily true; one truism does not imply the other. So again, what if we are in the wrong place, headed down the wrong road and have been for quite some time? Can we afford to continue to risk our future by making only a small adjustment with a left-hand or right-hand turn? Will that be enough? Have we been avoiding the truth all these years by thinking and acting in the way I did in my earlier driving example?

In order to answer these questions and before we can talk about a real solution, let's test the theory. We can take any topic that touches our lives every day and look at it in the light of my driving analogy. Let's use money as an example.

I have been a CPA in public practice for over 35 years. In the process I have dealt with many people regarding their money issues. For many folks, one of the biggest stumbling blocks to achieving financial security is their inability to admit they have made some very serious mistakes with their money. Some may go so far as to admit their mistake by saying they "could have made better choices," but that is as far as they will go in an admission of guilt.

Until they can assume responsibility for their error and change their thought process, finding a solution is almost impossible because they will probably continue to make the same mistakes. They refuse to consider the possibility that they are on the wrong road of beliefs and habits with regard to their money matters. Consequently, they will only consent to making some small changes in their planning and actions. Their thinking and their expectations will probably not change much as a result.

The second issue is even more difficult for people to consider. Starting over, going back to basics, and covering ground they have already covered, is a humbling thing. In many of my conversations with clients concerning their financial choices, I will hear them say something like, "I know, I know, I shouldn't have spent the money like I did. But it seemed right at the time and besides..." They are aware of their error. But the idea of going back to the beginning of the process and relearning the right way to proceed goes against their nature and requires a great deal of humility and patience. It is especially difficult for older people. They are embarrassed because they realize they are older and they should have known better.

And this ties in with a third issue. People usually try to avoid going back and relearning or re-experiencing a lesson. They would rather forget it and write it off to experience. They want to just keep moving forward thinking that somehow it will work out in the end. That is why filing for a form of bankruptcy is so popular. As the law is written, people get to keep a fair amount of what they have but also get to remove much of the debt they owe. So they can keep "moving forward" with a minimal amount of disruption to their life and way of thinking. In fact what they really need is significant changes to their spending and living habits. They are putting band-aids on their wounds when they need major surgery.

Anger is also a frequent component when money problems develop. It usually occurs because people don't like getting caught in an embarrassing situation. Men especially, who are often the ones in control of family finances, pride themselves on being savvy about money matters. Getting caught in a financial bind is frustrating and upsetting, to say the least. In some cases, it comes to light that one of the main reasons for the money problems may be that they secretly have been spending money on people and things they should never have allowed into their lives. Fear now joins with anger and embarrassment and makes a potent combination that is very resistant to the correct solution.

This brings us to another point: asking for help. In Alcoholics Anonymous, one of the prerequisites for joining the program is for a person to admit that they have a serious addiction problem. Then they need to realize that they cannot solve their addiction problem without outside help. Many people having financial difficulties will also be very reluctant to admit they have a serious problem and will look for help only as a last resort. But by then, most of the "band-aid solutions" are not going to work. They need "major surgery" at that point, and there still is no guarantee that the situation will get better. And, as with any kind of serious surgery, there is usually a lengthy recovery period.

The next point deals with the issue of control. People who are in charge of important matters such as business and family finances realize that they need to be in control in order for their financial wealth to grow. Control, in this case, is as important as having control when driving a car. As soon as a driver loses control, there will most likely be an accident and people may get hurt, or worse.

Frequently the person responsible for managing our money and handling our finances has a reputation for being good with money matters. It is expected that this person is reliable and diligent, and will not endanger the family or business. So if and when the person fails, that failure affects everyone by embarrassing us, destroying our trust, damaging our reputation and impacting our future. From that point forward, people question whether this person is trustworthy and capable of being in charge of the family or business finances.

As a result of these events, the person in charge may feel the need to make excuses for the failure. Excuses are very close cousins to lies and "misspoken words." The person will usually attempt to restore their formerly good reputation by trying to convince people that the money problem was not really their fault. Generally speaking, people know a lie or exaggeration when they hear one. In the end, the damage is done and the effort expended in attempting to regain one's former stature will fail or, at best, their abilities will be suspect.

Any of these issues can singlehandedly sabotage an honest effort at making a successful U-turn. They are that powerful, so it is no wonder how quickly and easily things can fall apart. However, there are ways of dealing successfully with these challenges. One of the ways to address our mistakes is by using "best practices".

As I mentioned earlier, many professionals utilize a concept called best practices in order to successfully manage their businesses as well as their personal lives. These best practices are a collection of policies, procedures and a moral code of ethics that together make up a generally accepted and approved way of managing a business. If we were to use that same methodology for dealing with life issues as mentioned above, what would be the best way to respond when faced with a series of problems that show we have made serious errors in judgment?

The first thing to do is to quickly accept responsibility for the failure. Analyze the problem and do everything possible to correct the situation. If it is necessary to go back to the beginning of a process in order to make things right, then do it. Lead the way in making the repairs. Set the example for others to follow, so that if they find themselves in a similar situation, they may remember your example.

Secondly, avoid the excuses and self-pity. Real leaders know when they have failed and will help guide others through the repair process even if they are the cause for the problem. Forward motion may have to stop until corrective action has been taken. But after that is done successfully, those involved can develop a new respect for that leader and for the corrective process.

In my experience, whenever I have purchased something that was faulty and found that it did not work, I appreciated the extra efforts of the seller to make it right. The same can be said when someone has hurt us on a personal level. It helps a great deal when that person comes to back to us, apologizes in person and does whatever it takes to undo the harm that was done. It seems that no one takes the time to do that anymore, but why? Because we are in a hurry these days, and, more to the point, we want to avoid confrontation and embarrassing situations, especially when they revolve around our personal failures.

These are some of the best practices people can follow in making a U-turn. Going back to fix, repair and restore something or someone is a very good thing, and down deep, most of us know this already. I do not think that any of the best practices mentioned above should surprise anyone. I could have easily applied these while I was lost and driving in circles in the story I told earlier, but I did not. Why didn't I?

Well, for one thing, my ego and my pride got in the way. In addition, my opinion of myself as a great driver had to be protected. There was no one in the car besides me who was going to take my side and that was the one thing that was very important to me. So I did all that I could to protect it including stretching the truth. I ended up making plenty of U-turns that night with the car. Instead I should have made one big U-turn in my attitude. It would have made the problem much easier to deal with.

When we start looking for evidence in the Bible concerning how difficult it is to make a U-turn, or how God might feel about our making U-turns, we quickly encounter one of the major themes of the Scriptures. In biblical language it is referred to as repentance. I mentioned it in an earlier chapter but we need to discuss it in greater detail. In essence, making a U-turn is a contemporary way of saying that a person is repentant.

John the Baptist is probably the most famous of all biblical figures who preached about this topic frequently. He was the one chosen to announce to the public at large that a Savior would soon be coming. John quoted Isaiah in his message:

> *In those days John the Baptist came, preaching in the Desert of Judea and saying, "Repent, for the kingdom of heaven is near." This is he who was spoken of through the prophet Isaiah:*
> *"A voice of one calling in the desert. Prepare the way for the Lord, make straight paths for him."*
> *"I baptize you with water for repentance. But after me will come one who is more powerful than I, whose sandals I am not fit to carry. He will baptize you with the Holy Spirit and with fire."* (Matthew 3:1-3 and 11-12)

The Savior he spoke of was, of course, Jesus Christ. Making a straight path for Christ's arrival was John's way of telling his listeners (and us for that matter) that we are to stop sinning and to change our ways. We are to turn from our bad habits and straighten out our lives. Incidentally, is it not interesting how that concept of making a straight path ties in nicely with Jeremiah 6:16 quoted in Chapter 1? *"....ask for the ancient paths, ask where the good way is, and walk in it."* The straight path would be the best path, a good way to travel. In order to get onto that path we would have to face all of our sins and bad habits and resolve never to return to committing them.

Most people misunderstand the core elements of true repentance. It is true that in order to be repentant, one must be honestly sorry for one's sins. But sorrow alone is not enough. Action is required. In other words, having true sorrow for something we did that hurt someone is a good thing, and apologizing and making reparations to the person is also a very necessary part of successfully completing the process of repentance. But to have true repentance, we need a change of heart, a change in the way we think and behave. So in addition to apologies and making amends, the offensive behavior has to cease. A new behavior, motivated by our new thinking, must take its place, and a new heading or course change in our future actions must be taken. In short, we need to make a 180-degree turn, otherwise known as a U-turn. We have to stop heading in the direction that was characterized by our bad behavior.

Listen to the following story that Jesus told:

> *"What do you think? There was a man who had two sons. He went to the first and said, 'Son, go and work today in the vineyard.'*
> *'I will not,' he answered, but later he changed his mind and went.*
> *Then the father went to the other son and said the same thing. He answered, 'I will, sir,' but he did not go. Which of the two did what his father wanted?"*
> *"The first." they answered.*
> *Jesus said to them, "I tell you the truth, the tax collectors and the prostitutes are entering the kingdom of God ahead of you. For John came to you to show you the way of righteousness, and you did not believe him, but the tax collectors and the prostitutes did. And even after you saw this, you did not repent and believe him".*
> (Matthew 21:28-32 emphasis added)

Christ was explaining to His listeners that what a person does in the end is most important. The first son in the story said no to his father's request and appeared to go his own way regardless of what his father wanted. But after he thought about it, he made the U-turn and did what was right. Jesus said that this was pleasing to God despite the son's earlier disobedience.

The second son, however, sounded very compliant at first and declared that he would do what the father wanted, but in the end he disappointed his father. He not only did not do what the father wanted, but he was also guilty of lying to his father, making matters worse. The latter son is likened to many of us who hear the Word of God but do not alter our lifestyles to accommodate and adapt that Word into our daily routines.

We may change a few of the smaller things we do each day to better comply with God's laws, but in doing so we probably do not address the more important issues. As long as we leave out the more important issues, we risk ending up in the same situation as the rich young ruler that we spoke of in Chapter 2. As is always the case with God, the consequence of refusing to make the U-turn can be devastating.

Remember this: in God's eyes, how you start is not as important as how you finish.

At this point I am hoping you are beginning to appreciate how difficult it can be for any of us to make a real and permanent U-turn in our lives. There usually is a great deal to consider, not the least of which are the issues I have listed above. You might want to keep this notion of repentance in the back of your mind as we continue to talk about U-turns. As I said, in reality they are one and the same thing.

*"Treat everyone with politeness, even those who are rude to you - not because they are nice, but because you are."*

~ Unknown

# 6

## What Happened?
## How Did We Get So Far Off
## the Right Road?

*"Tell me and I'll forget; show me and I may remember;
involve me and I'll understand."*

~ Chinese Proverb

I have a good friend who is an amateur sailor and owns his own sailboat. He told me about a one-day sailing trip he had taken with his wife. He was planning to cross Long Island Sound to gain a port on the other side. But he had to cross the Sound at a diagonal angle, making the trip longer and a bit more difficult. It would have been easier, navigationally, to just head directly south across the 25 miles of water and then cut east for another 20 miles or so. But he decided to take the shorter diagonal southeast route. He said that he eventually got there, but for every minute of that over-five-hour journey, he had to keep checking his heading and making adjustments and corrections.

Why? Because the action of the waves, currents, and the wind which at times comes directly against the boat and at times crosswise to it, kept pushing him off course. He also had to watch out for rocks, shallow water, sandbars, boaters, fishermen, swimmers and more. It was real work to stay on the right course and he could not lose focus for even a minute.

This story can be a great metaphor for life. It is not easy to make our way in life each day. There are lots of forces that are trying to get us off course and keep us there. But beyond the difficulty of keeping our heading fixed in the right direction, there is something else that can get us off track.

I remember that old song from years past entitled, "*How You Gonna Keep Them Down on the Farm, After They've Seen Paris?*" That title sums up where we find ourselves today. The fact is that many of us have left "the farm" much like the Prodigal Son did, and have gone off to do whatever seems to be more fun and profitable. The farm may have been a boring place, but it was a safe place and we knew we could rely on it always being there for us.

Over the last 50 years or so there have been many notable events in our cultural history, both good and bad. At the core of these events have been a number of key factors that conspired to get us off the road for right living. In general, the first half of the 20th century was plagued by two World Wars, the stock market crash of 1929 and the Great Depression of the 1930's. Those events shook the world and disrupted the lives of millions. They also left a permanent scar on many people who lived through those times.

So, at the doorstep of the 1950's, we as a country were ready to break loose and enjoy life. I remember my parents and others of their generation saying that they wanted us young folks to have what they could never have while growing up as kids. They wanted "the good life" for their children.

This quest for the good life gave rise to a wave of consumerism never before seen in all of history. Remember the phrase "keeping up with the Jones'?" Manufacturers and producers were falling all over themselves to offer us all of the modern conveniences and other trappings of the good life. Some people were, in all seriousness, competing with their neighbors in trying to be the first ones on their block with the newest cars, appliances, televisions, and other things.

But people needed a way to pay for all of these things. So the financial services industry came up with the concept of personal consumer financing, such as car loans and boat loans. They expanded the standard concept of mortgages and personal loans, to include payment plans for other household or personal items with credit cards and the like. The technology industry also joined the movement, seeing it as an opportunity for greater profits, and went to work to develop and create the new items people would want to have in their homes. As a result, every year we looked forward to a new and improved version of the same product. The progress was simply amazing and it gave us all the sense that we were really making advancement in society's growth and development.

Some current-day historians and economists think of this period as the perfect storm of consumer events. We had access to the items we wanted most, technology was ever-evolving and yielding an inventory of new things to buy, and we had personal credit to pay for it all. We could have the things we wanted right away by borrowing from our future earnings. And that was all good. After all, we were living in a powerful and growing country and felt that we would always have our jobs, and even more money to pay for what we desired. Success in our future was a sure thing. Besides, we deserved it. We just helped save the world from the threat of takeover by Germany and Japan! This combination proved to be too much of a temptation for many people.

The emergence of the Internet toward the end of the 20th century acted as a catalyst, facilitating the acquisition of more things, all the while increasing the levels of accompanying debt. The results speak for themselves. We were lured "off the farm," so to speak, and many of us have never looked back until this day.

Consider a critical Scripture reference that relates perfectly to this discussion. The New Testament writer Timothy was talking about the love of money and piling up all the kinds of things money can buy. He had this to say:

> *People who want to get rich fall into temptation and a trap and into many foolish and harmful desires that plunge men into ruin and destruction. For the love of money is a root of all kinds of evil. Some people, eager for money, have wandered from the faith and pierced themselves with many griefs.* (1 Timothy 6:8-10)

As an aside, I am always amazed at people who scoff at the Bible and claim that it cannot be relied on for answers to today's modern problems. A person can take any issue that we humans face on a daily basis and search the Scriptures for guidance and they will find the answers. They may not like what they read but the answers are certainly there. This fact alone is proof that God's Word is very relevant, even for us today. We who do not listen to that Word are foolish, to say the very least. Human nature has not changed much in the past several thousand years. There is a great deal of truth in the Scriptures. They can literally forecast what we are likely to do as humans regardless of our generation or technological advances that may have occurred.

We can look at Timothy's words and see that people today still pursue money as they did long ago, almost to the exclusion of all else. This pursuit can destroy a person and even those closest to them. Simply put, we are like children when it comes to wanting things. Many of us seem to have that weakness built into our DNA. Consequently, it is relatively easy to stray off course and get lost. And the longer we continue to stray, the further we go from where we should be living and working.

Think back to the story of Adam and Eve in the Garden of Eden. They too failed to listen to God's command not to eat from that one special tree in the Garden. They heard and understood God's instruction, but they chose not to comply with it. They had access to everything that they could have wanted in the Garden, but still they could not resist the temptation of that one forbidden item. Look at what happened.

Some people laugh at the notion of a garden such as the one in that story. The point is not whether there really was a garden, but rather that the innately human behavior of so long ago was pretty much the same as it is today. The consequences of the actions in the Garden affected future generations. It is the same for us today. The consequences of our non-compliance with God's laws can also affect us and our children. This story is a warning to those who have enough sense to hear it and believe the message.

The reasons for how we got so far off course are very important, for if and when we do decide to make a U-turn in our life, we will need to know the warning signs when we might start to veer off the correct road. Once again, my friend, sailing his boat across the Sound, was well aware of how easily he could get off course. But he was prepared for it. Yes, he had to watch not only for the forces that would push him away from his destination, but he also had to know what to do, not *if* but, *when* he strayed off course again. He had the knowledge and the equipment to handle the task.

Let me explain this another way. If we could see the daily

lives of everyone in our society laid out on a vast plain where we work, live, recreate, raise our families and so on, we would see that there are designated lanes of movement for people much like traffic on a highway or freeway. These lanes have developed over the years from generally accepted rules of behavior in society and grew into accepted pathways along which people can live their lives successfully. Somewhere back in the 1950's and 1960's, members of our Boomer generation looked at those pathways and decided that they were too restrictive and obsolete.

Additionally we found out that much of the "good stuff" and the freedoms we wanted seemed to be on the other side of the established boundaries and pathways. Many of us reasoned that the fencing had to come down in order to give us access.

So we rebelled against the established rules and customs and began to dismantle the fencing that marked the lanes and that kept order. What many of us did not realize at the time was that the fencing was there to also protect us from harm. Consequentially many have been hurt because they strayed beyond the boundaries and safe zones established by those who came before us. Those who established these pathways were our parents, grandparents and their ancestors. The lanes developed as a result of their sticking to the best practices of living that worked for them. My earlier list of statistics on negative events that have occurred on our generational watch, as we tried to disregard their best practices, is proof that we did a great disservice not only to ourselves but also to those younger than us.

Our generation wanted the freedom to pick and choose what we wanted in life, and to be able to access it when we wanted it. Many wanted things like free sex, free drugs, the ability to get high whenever they wished, etc., and we also wanted to be rid of the outdated and constrictive norms that society had

94

established over many years. So we worked very hard at taking down the fencing that held us back. Gatherings such as the one at Woodstock in 1969 made our feelings and beliefs abundantly clear. For that reason, Woodstock became the *de facto* corporate image of our generation.

Generation X, which followed the Boomer generation, looked at what we were doing and some decided to join us in dismantling those guideposts for living. Now, if we flash forward to today at the beginning of the 21st century, the newest generation of Millennials is surveying that same vast plain trying to figure out what is the best way to proceed in order to successfully live their lives. Many have grown up in homes ravaged by divorce, addictions, and money problems, and they don't want to repeat those experiences for themselves.

But the "safe and recommended pathways" are mostly gone from sight now. The fencing is down and much of it has been removed. Consequently, many people have gone far off the right path. Since this has happened, the business world, including whole industries, has had to develop a concept called Business Ethics at the corporate level. It establishes acceptable codes of conduct for their respective employees and business owners. Since generally accepted moral standards and virtues have long been in decline in the universal population, professionals especially have had to develop these sets of recommended behaviors. Many industries have even incorporated penalties and fines for those who break these rules.

These developments have made it even more difficult for young people to understand what is right and wrong. For example, if you are a doctor, you must behave according to a designated set of moral codes as promoted by groups such as the American Medical Association. But if you drive a truck, your industry's code may be very different. It could be much less restrictive or even more limiting. Why the vast difference? How will young people know which behavior is allowed in which industry or part of society? Moral right and wrong used to be known to all of us in the general population and applicable in virtually all situations. Current thinking tells us that it "depends on the circumstances."

The truth is, we have allowed the concept of "truth" to escape us. When we allowed the fencing, as I refer to it, to be removed, the truth went with it. The fencing was constructed and placed into position by the generations that came before us. They knew what real truth was as it related to the real world. They were not arbitrary in their construction of those guide posts and accepted pathways.

These societal boundaries were created with great attention paid to the concept and existence of absolute truths, as well as the result of years of experience with what works best. Best practices is not a new concept or something that we discovered in the last few years or decades. It has been around for a very long time in one form or another and our ancestors utilized best practices in the construction of those pathways. In days of old, young people would learn from their parents and older folks how best to live. Wisdom usually came from grandparents and those who have seen a great deal of life.

Not very long ago in our country, there were the concepts of good, better, best, and worst. We as Americans always sought the best for ourselves and our families regardless of the issue at hand. Sometimes we could not afford the best, and so we settled for the "better" option or if necessary, simply a "good" choice. We never considered accepting a bad or the worst choice; it simply would not do for us Americans.

At a time when we were being honest with ourselves, we knew that the best way to complete a job or obtain something we wanted was to work hard for it. That truth carried the day; our parents and grandparents taught us the importance of that truth and constantly reinforced it by setting the example themselves. We knew that there was usually only one way to complete our work: the right way, so that the item we produced would work properly or the service we performed would be reliable.

But now, without the established pathways and fencing to guide us, many of us have gotten the clear impression that there are any number of ways to obtain and produce what we want and all of them are "good enough" ways, if not the best ways. In other words, the best way to live is now available to us in a number of different sizes, shapes, colors, and methods. The truth now seems to come in many variations. We are told that there are numerous other pathways we can take to get to our desired destination and each is as valid as the other. It's my belief that this change in our thinking is the direct result of living in a consumerist mode for so many years. But the question very few people are asking is whether each way is equal in effectiveness and results. Is this new multi-based interpretation of the truth working well for us?

As I mentioned earlier, taking down the fencing had another perceived benefit to us as well. It allowed our generation to pursue the things we wanted that were outside the old established pathways. We could now have that second home, the more expensive car, or more of the kind of food we really loved, the divorce we needed, the drugs we craved, and more. Many physical and societal restrictions were being removed for the most part, and we were like kids let loose in a candy shop with no authority figure to tell us what we could or couldn't have.

From time to time you hear the phrase, "the truth is..." and that statement in itself points to something fewer and fewer believe. Absolute truth does still exist in the world. If you do not believe me, then take a look at the natural world. The entire world around us still operates on the same exact set of absolute truths that were in place thousands of years ago.

We are the only creatures in the universe that have decided that we can suspend the truth about a given matter when it is perceived to be for our personal advantage or need. We have long demanded that we hold the "trump card" giving us that right. For the golfers reading this, it would be like playing a round of golf and taking a "mulligan" (a "do over" shot that does not count toward your score) whenever you want. For that matter, why not put eraser at the end of the scoring pencil? Wouldn't that be easier? But real life doesn't work that way; we only wish it did.

When we follow real truth, we end up with the best results concerning whatever the topic or issue is at hand. When we do not follow it, or worse, when we no longer know what the truth is, we lose our direction. We will get lost and will probably stray far from the correct road or path. When you use a GPS unit in a car, the unit gives you the truth about your location at any time. It gives you the truth about your heading, any upcoming detour information and more. Isn't that what we want from our GPS unit? We want the truth. When I visit my doctor, I want him or her to give me the truth and nothing less. Ironically, we get very upset when others lie to us. But we seem to be comfortable with lying to ourselves and to others about things we are doing that are clearly wrong.

We need the truth to live correctly and move in the right

direction. Without it, we are lost. So, what have we done to those in the generations that will follow us? Have we given them the truth? Or have we taken it from them? Have we confused them by giving them many versions of the truth?

I recall sitting there at that AA meeting, watching all of those young people struggling to get their lives back, and concluding that we older folks have a great deal of work to do. We need to go back and help them and others like them avoid making the same mistakes over and over again. How many more divorces, abortions, bankruptcies or drug addictions do we need to convince us that we are on the wrong road? It seems generation after generation continues to make the same errors over and over. It is insane and we are not doing enough to break the cycle.

We should know by now how divorce occurs, how bankruptcy happens, how smoking leads to cancer, etc. But generation after generation continues to experience these tragic events first-hand. They work at reinventing the wheel, so to speak, over and over again. It's the *learning by burning* routine. And many of us older folks seem to be content to watch them go through this process. The pain and suffering is just as destructive each successive time it happens.

But even if we decide to make the U-turn in order to help change things, what will we tell the people we encounter? What is the truth? Where can we find it without exception? What is a reliable source?

We in the Boomer generation have grown up thinking that anything new is better, more advanced, of greater value and quality than anything made by, or even believed by, older generations. The truth, we claim, must therefore be found in these newer products and ways of living and thinking. Many of us have come to believe that the truth in any situation evolves as our lives evolve each day. Really? Do we honestly think that God would agree with us on that point? Does nature work that way?

Some call it evolution, but what is evolving? Does the truth ever change or evolve? Or is it the earthly matter and material that truth works with that changes? The human body has evolved to some extent, for example, but the truths that govern *how* it works remains the same. How nature functions is basically the same today as it was thousands of years ago. It goes through cycles, but it still balances out and life is sustained.

If a doctor from the 21st century could go back in time, he or she we be able to treat a sick person in 4000 BC with medicine and procedures from today's world. Our medicines and techniques would be more effective than those of that time, and the treatments would have much of the same effect as they do today. The patient would probably respond favorably to the treatment, because our physiology hasn't changed all that much over that span of time.

If there is a God, and many of us believe there is, then there will be a final day when we meet Him. Then we will know the truth for sure. Can we afford to wait until then to discover it? Are you willing to wait until then? I am not. I refuse to gamble with my eternal life, especially when we already have the Bible to guide us and years of accumulated human experience to tell us what works best. Whenever the topic comes up about the genuineness and truth of the Scriptures, people conveniently forget that many millions of people have died over the years believing and defending the truths found in the Scriptures. Could they all have been wrong or misguided?

Consider this example. Many people think that books written today have greater wisdom and value than books of 100 years ago. How do we know that? Browse the shelves of any bookstore and see how many titles are in stock with original publication dates older than five to seven years. People, for the most part, do not want old books, they want new books.

Some people question whether or not older people can advise young people today because things are so different now than when the older folks were their age. I think we all know the answer to that one. I have visited many of my clients in nursing homes over the years and have been disappointed that these people are not actively sought out for their experience and advice. They have gone through life and have encountered many of the situations that trouble us today, but we do not see them as a valuable resource. I feel that this is an incredible waste. Discovering the many truths about life has taken them their whole lives and many of us seem to feel that what they have learned cannot be valuable to us. So we avoid them and put them in "community warehouses" where they can quietly live out their lives. Yes, I called this a waste, but I think a better way to describe it is as a *capital sin against God*.

Here is where we are today: we would like to know how we, as a society, have gotten so far from the truth. How could we be so far from where we should be by now? The answer can be found once we make up our mind about God. Simply put, the decision concerning whether real absolute truth exists or not rests fundamentally on whether we think there is a God or not. If we believe there is no deity behind all of creation, then truth must come from a source here on earth. And since humans are the highest form of life on our planet, then it is logical that humans get to decide what the truth is and is not.

But again, as with everything else in life, we do not want to be restrained or restricted in making those decisions. We want the ability to change our minds about any topic particularly as we see conditions changing in our culture or our personal lives. The same can be said about our attitude toward truth; we want the ability to change the truth as well so it can best meet our personal needs. We never did like the kind of truth for which "one size fits all."

If we do not honestly believe in God, then I guess this line of reasoning makes sense. In this scenario, we take God's place and we get to decide all of the weightier matters as we see fit. So if we want 2+2 to be 5 for a while instead of 4, then why not allow it? After all, under these circumstances it is solely up to us; we are the ultimate users and have the ultimate authority.

However, if we believe there is a God that created all of the cosmos and the earth, and everything in and around it, including us, then it would be absurd to think that He did not give us instructions for living the best life possible. For that matter, could God create all of this without having a basic set of rules, laws and truths in place? When we look at every aspect of nature, we see something that operates with great precision, control and regularity. We set our clocks by the movements of planetary bodies. The seasons all follow each other on schedule and each species of wildlife procreates and lives basically in the same manner year after year. There is no new, improved or upgraded version of nature each year. The earth rotates around the sun the same way day in, day out and there is no way we can improve on that system.

So then, if we believe in God, is it logical to think that he would make humans according to a different system of creation? Biologically speaking, much in the makeup of our bodies is compatible with nature. We are made from the same components found throughout nature. Again, would He create us and then not give us directions on how best to live? He gave His creations in the animal kingdom instinct to help guide them in their survival. Instinct, to them, is a form of the truth that helps them live the best and safest lives possible.

To us He gave free will to choose what is good and bad and the ability to follow our decisions through to the end. He also gave us the ability to learn and grow. But what good is free will if you have so many choices presented to you but no knowledge of what is best and how to safely select the right choice? One of our choices has to be the truth, and it is most logical that He would have given us that truth as well. The rest, then, is up to us. We must choose wisely.

If there are no truths that can always be relied on, to correlate with the natural world around us and even with the eternal life beyond this world, then we are essentially in the same position as all of the animal kingdom. We are, by all accounts, the greatest creation on planet earth, perhaps even in the universe. Scientifically, our bodies are marvels in how they work and they stand as proof of that fact. Again, if there is a God, I would think He would take even better care of His greatest creation by giving us a set of eternal truths to live by.

Think about this; it is very important. When you bring your car to a mechanic for a repair, how do you want him or her to fix it? I would think you would want them to repair the car using the best parts and with the best repair methods available. The mechanic should rely on his knowledge of industry best practices and techniques to accomplish the best result possible. Ideally these same methods are applied every day in every industry. Why should we not have the same concept for living the best possible lives available to us? Does it not make sense to look back for the old ways, and the best ways, to raise children, control our urges, maintain our diets, succeed in our jobs, conduct our lives and later pass these along to our children? That's what Tom, the twelve-year-old I mentioned earlier, wanted me to provide to him.

The bottom line is that if we believe in God, then there has to be a set of best practices for successful living that would have come from our Creator. And these practices would not be open to discussion or modification. As is the case with all of nature, it works, it operates, and it continues to produce according to the old ways and established physical laws of nature that have been in place for centuries. I believe human beings are also subject to a similar system. We just have to rediscover it. As someone once said concerning moral issues and right living: "Everything that is important is already known. All we have to do is rediscover it."

If we agree that we are on the wrong road, that we are heading in the wrong direction and that we need to make a big change by turning around and going back, then we need to question everything that got us to where we are now. If we do not know what is right and what is wrong, then making a U-turn will probably not help much. We will only continue to use the same belief system we used all along that got us lost in the first place.

That's exactly what happened to me that night we were trying to get to the party. I kept making U-turns in an effort to correct my wrong heading. But because I didn't know the correct direction to head in, I had to make more and more U-turns in my car. Remember this, two consecutive U-turns make a complete circle. If you do not have your directions right to begin with, you will just end up going in circles because you will just be making U-turn after U-turn.

We need a new GPS system. If the old one got us lost to begin with, then we have to replace it. We need to re-examine what we are using for "life maps" — core values and foundational principles. I believe we have to relearn real truth and we have to go back and find out what real truth is regardless of any of our preconceived feelings and notions. And we need to do this before we start making any major life U-turns.

If you look up the definition of the word "anarchy" you may see an explanation such as the following from Wikipedia:

*A social state in which there is no governing person or group of people, but each individual has absolute liberty (without the implication of disorder), but is bound by a social code.*

When I found this definition I began to realize how close we are to this state of living. When we lose absolute truth, we then have to accept whatever people want the truth to be and that means there will also be a struggle for control. At the very least, the definition of truth in various matters will be changing often. That will lead to instability, chaos and sin. Anarchy can be dangerous, and if we do not restore the concept and knowledge of absolute truth to our lives, society, as we now know it, will be lost. Don't think that this is an unlikely possibility here in America. Elsewhere, history has proven that it can happen very easily. Our arrogance will not preclude that event from happening here.

Many historians believe that our fall is inevitable. All of the ancient empires and societies, from the Romans and Greeks to the Mayans, Egyptians, Aztecs and others, eventually collapsed. Who are we to think that we can easily continue to live as we want and not be subject to the same outcome as predecessor societies? There is only One who can save us now but we have to turn to Him. We need to make a big U-turn and we need to make it now.

Compare the above concept of anarchy to what Jeremiah told us and see which one gives you more comfort.

> *This is what the LORD says:*
> *Stand at the crossroads and look;*
> *ask for the ancient paths,*
> *ask where the good way is, and walk in it,*
> *and you will find rest for your souls.*　　(Jeremiah 6:16)

Let's now take a look at what has happened to the concept of real truth in our culture and personal lives. It will help us get a better idea of what we must know and what must be done if and when we decide to make that U-turn.

*"Things turn out best for the people who make the best out of the way things turn out."*

~ John R. Wooden (1910 -);
retired basketball coach, author

# 7

## The Truth Is...

*"Nobody is bored when he is trying to make something that is beautiful, or to discover something that is true. "*

~ William Inge (1913-1973);
American playwright

"The truth is..." We might hear these three words when someone is about to become very honest with us. The occasion usually concerns an important issue when they are ready to confess something they did wrong. The circumstances may differ but they know they have been caught in a lie or misrepresentation and now they must to tell the truth about the issue at hand. In the last chapter we discussed how easily we can get off the right road when considering what real truth is and is not. We found that as we start to distort or "customize" the truth to fit our "evolving" lives and needs, we begin to move off the correct path and onto other risk-filled pathways. Usually we do this because it may, at first, seem to better suit our desires. However, our perception of the better road can change very quickly.

The major question we face is how to discern the real truth in any given situation. Where can we go to find the real facts about a certain issue or aspect of life that will help us make the right decision? Is there a single source or a great variety of options available to us concerning truth? Once again, we're back to that question that 12-year-old Tom asked me at the party I spoke of earlier.

In order to make a U-turn and see the effort yield permanent success, I believe we need to know what is absolutely true about truth. As I said earlier, real truth about any topic in our lives has to come from one of two sources. It must come from either outside of this world, from a supernatural source, or it must come from somewhere within our world or a human source.

If there is no God, and therefore no supernatural life beyond this one, then truth has to come from a human source. In this case we can live our lives as we please because there is nothing or no one to whom we are accountable after this life. The truth can then become whatever we want and declare it to be.

If we believe there is no God, then the truth also needs to be something flexible and adaptable that will serve us and suit our personal needs, as opposed to us being compliant and subservient to a greater power. If there is no God, then we are the ultimate authority. In a sense we replace Him in the grand scheme of life. We become god, if you will. So you can do as you please, live as you like and if you plan on breaking established rules and laws, just make sure you do not get caught by any of our government's law enforcement agencies. That would be how many of us would live if we truly believed there was no God. Interestingly, many do live that way even though they claim to believe in God.

On the other hand, if we feel that there is a God who created all that we see and experience, and we are certain that there is a life after this one, then there must exist certain rules and laws created by God that regulate the life around us, as well as the life to come. Either there is a God or there is not. If there is, then He is the ultimate authority and we should follow His rules and look for His wisdom and guidance. In the end, He is the one who hands out the final grades, so to speak.

This discussion plays a very important part in our plan to make a U-turn. If we decide to go back and fix whatever we did wrong in the past, or even if we decide to help correct something that someone else did wrong, we had better know the truth about what we are trying to accomplish. By going back or involving ourselves in other peoples' problems, we will probably cause a stir and perhaps even distress for the people we confront.

Remember, when we discover what real truth is and we try to bring that message to others, there is a high probability that they will not accept it. In most cases people have been living their lives a certain way for many years. Their beliefs are based solidly in their life experiences, and they will most likely be unwilling to change those beliefs. They will guard their beliefs and fight to keep them. People can become territorial about their way of thinking and will defend their personal beliefs fiercely.

Few of us take the time to really question our long-held beliefs. People are reluctant to consider that some of the things they have thought to be true for so many years are, in fact, wrong. We have to be ready to deal with rejection and make sure we come prepared to explain the truth in a loving and convincing way. We will need evidence and convincing arguments. Here's an interesting passage that few people know:

> *With many similar parables Jesus spoke the word to them, as much as they could understand. He did not say anything to them without using a parable. But when he was alone with his own disciples, he explained everything.* (Mark 4:33-34)

Even Jesus had to spend time alone with His disciples to explain the truth in detail. We can just imagine what those conversations must have been like. The disciples witnessed incredible things with Christ. But performing miracles was not enough; Jesus had to explain things to them as well. That may give us some indication of the work that is before us.

We will want to make sure that we have the real truth, that we understand it well enough to explain it, and that we can lead others to where God wants them to be. Without the truth, even as we begin, we will fail. Without the truth, we will probably continue to operate under our same old belief system, and nothing will have changed from our old perspective. We will use the same techniques, expend the same amount of energy, and make the same old tired arguments as to why we are right and someone else is wrong. In addition, it we fail to recognize the truth, the people we encounter will most likely expect us to make our same old tired arguments. If we revert to those old arguments, it will probably shut down any meaningful discussion, and we will only succeed in making a bad situation worse.

From a logical point of view, as I look at the facts, I have to conclude that there is a God. There is too much evidence of supernatural design in all that surrounds us. Our bodies merge with nature in all that we do. That means that we are part of nature, a very large part. And since there is evidence of great design and control in nature, then there must also exist design and control as they relate to human existence. It therefore must be that the God of the Bible does exist. Why? Simply put, there just does not seem to be any other supernatural force that could be powerful enough, benign enough, charitable enough and patient enough to put up with our behavior for so long.

Another kind of god would have probably destroyed us all by now. Neither are there claims that any other god came to earth to sacrifice himself for our benefit. That is what ultimately separates the God of the Bible from all other gods. The story of Jesus Christ, and His birth, His life and teachings, His death and His subsequent resurrection are all part of an incredible story. That story is based on an ultimate and unconditional love for His creation, us. This makes the most sense to me, so I accept it as being true.

I believe that He did give us the instructions we need for right living in the form of His Holy Scriptures and that He sends His Holy Spirit to help guide us every day, if we choose to listen. When we look at how nature operates each second of every day, we have to conclude that it does so with great regularity and is subject to great control. Even after nature goes on a rampage with volcanic eruptions, tsunamis, hurricanes and such, the environment returns to a balanced position, every time. The world does not end even after the tragedy caused by an earthquake or flood. Again, the system has to have been designed by a Creator; there is too much evidence of complicated construction, operation, control and purpose. To trust all of what we see in our world simply to the chance and random operation of evolution requires a different level of faith — blind faith — a willingness to ignore the proof surrounding us that there is a single supernatural Creator!

Let's go a bit further with the assumption that there is a God. Where then can we go to find truth? Is there a single source or at least a place to start?

Let's begin with what Jesus Himself said:

*To the Jews who had believed him, Jesus said, "If you hold to my teaching, you are really my disciples. Then you will know the truth, and the truth will set you free."*
(John 8:31-32)

When Jesus appeared on earth a couple of thousand years ago, He presented us with a huge dilemma. We had to either believe He was (and still is) God or He was not God. Interestingly, there is no way to prove it beyond a doubt either way; even Christ Himself did not prove it. The Gospels speak about all of His miracles and good works. They tell us of what He advised us to do and believe. But in the end, after all of His good deeds and efforts, the people of His day voted to kill Him, and they did so. From that perspective, He Himself failed to convince the majority of His contemporaries that He was God.

The verse from John's Gospel leaves no room for misunderstanding with regard to the issue of truth and where it may be found. Jesus claims to be the source of all truth.

However, there is no way for us to prove it. That is why we call faith "faith." Christ's claim has to be taken on faith. The nature of faith is to believe in things we cannot touch or verify with our human senses.

He said that if we hold to all of His teachings, then what we learn (the truth) will set us free. That means we will be free, not to do whatever we want, but free to follow Christ and do what He wants. In return we will receive His protection, guidance, access to eternal life and His help in preventing us from falling into sin, thereby suffering its consequences.

If you therefore believe in God, does it not make sense to look to Him as the ultimate source of truth? Some people say that the Scriptures were written too long ago and are for another time and place in history. They contend that our time and place today is very different than that of thousands of years ago, so as to render any advice they offer obsolete or impractical.

We must understand that the Scriptures were not written for any specific time and place. They were written for people, as a guide for human behavior. It is reasonably clear that human behavior has not changed very much over the passage of many years. God knew that and that is why the Bible does not contain any technical designs or drawings describing how to build a "better mousetrap" for example. God's focus was on helping all people for all time to learn how to live correctly. If at the time of their writing, the instructions were being given only for the people of the day, then we would have received more updated instructions over the years.

The Scriptures are timeless. They will still be true even in the next life. As a matter of fact, they contain the laws, rules and literal picture of what life will be like in Heaven. Here is an interesting thought: if everyone on earth suddenly decided to comply with everything Christ set out in the Gospels, would we not have Heaven here on earth?

What we call Heaven is already described in the Bible. Everything Christ told us already exists in Heaven. If we will not listen to Him now, and do what He says now, then why should we expect to go to Heaven later on? It is fair to ask why you would want to. If we do not want Heaven here and now, then logically we will not want it later.

So it is by our choices in this life that we accept or reject the kind of existence God has prepared for us in the next life. He has created Heaven for us. Do you want to go there when you die? If your answer is yes, then it is logical that we start to live by His Word now. Live out His truth in your life today so that it will be a simple step to pass from the here and now through the crossover point at death into that glorious future with Him. This approach makes the most sense to me and I treat it as a given truth I can rely on.

Consider the next passage where Christ is speaking to His

Father about His disciples. He refers to us in the present day in the subsequent passage:

> *They are not of the world, even as I am not of it.*
> *Sanctify them by the truth; your word is truth. As you*
> *sent me into the world, I have sent them into the world.*
>
> (John 17:16-17)

> *My prayer is not for them alone. I pray also for those*
> *who will believe in me through their message, that all of*
> *them may be one, Father, just as you are in me and I am*
> *in you. May they also be in us so that the world may*
> *believe that you have sent me.* (John 17:20-22)

Jesus asks God to sanctify His disciples, to set them aside as holy people, and to make them clean for a sacred use. He was also suggesting that this could be done by their knowing and applying the truth in their lives. God's Word is the truth. If we decide to make a U-turn in our lives, we want to be successful; we do not want our efforts to take us even further in the wrong direction. Looking to God for His help at this time and for this task is critical.

Just as Jesus did, we too are asking Him to sanctify us, to make us holy and pure so that as we move through our lives, the impact we have on others is totally based in truth. A great example of this precept can be found in the Alcoholics Anonymous 12-step program which stresses the need to believe in a "higher power" and the need to turn our lives over to Him so that He may, in a sense, sanctify us and our efforts at restoring our health. It is a classic example of making a U-turn.

Beyond this first, all-important realization that God is the source of all truth, there are other steps we can take to help us find the truth. These include:

1) Examining what has worked well in the past, not only in our lives but in other peoples' lives. We can also do the research online. We can ask family members, friends and others whom we trust for their advice. Once again we refer to best practices as they relate to our lives. Talk with your older friends and folks in your families; they could provide you with great wisdom gained from experience. Don't be afraid to take notes!

2) Searching the Scriptures and reading the commentaries on the related verses. Now that we know God's Word is the truth, we can study it. By the way, what most people don't realize is that, as we read Scripture, it is not only the words that are sacred and effective, it is God's Holy Spirit helping us to comprehend the meaning of the words.

When Jesus left to return to Heaven He said He would send us a "helper," His Holy Spirit, so that He would be with us until the end. When you open the Bible to read and learn, you automatically have the most learned tutor in all the universe to help you. And if you let Him, He will accompany you as you apply what you have learned to your life.

3) Using your common sense. Have you ever wondered why some people seem to be blessed with an overabundance of common sense? Where do they get it ? Why

do we have such a hard time figuring out what to do about certain situations in our lives while these people seem to work through the same difficult issues with great ease and confidence? I am convinced that the gift we call common sense is really the influence of the Holy Spirit in our lives. When we let God into our lives and ask Him to walk with us, to talk to us, to protect and care for us, He really does! We account for the resulting effect as common sense but in reality, it is oftentimes God's Spirit.

4) Praying. If there is a God, then He is most certainly aware of us. He made us. We are His children and as such He is constantly concerned about our needs and welfare. Talk to Him about anything at any time. A friend told me a story about her aging mother who lived in Florida. My friend began receiving phone calls from concerned friends of her mother. They told her that they had been seeing her mother talking to herself, out loud, while driving and walking around town. They witnessed this behavior even when she had been home all alone. My friend was worried and decided to take away her mother's car keys. When her mother asked why she was doing this, my friend told her about how she had been seen talking to herself quite frequently. Her mother responded with, "Oh that! I'm not talking to myself. I'm talking to Jesus. He is with me all the time now. I depend on Him for advice and help and it really works!" My friend learned an important lesson that day. Her mother made an important U-turn in her life, and it had a profound effect both on her and her daughter.

5) Finally, going to the Book of Proverbs in the Bible. Very few people realize how much practical wisdom is located in that one book. As you read the verses you will see in the margins the references to other parts of the Bible as they relate to the topics in Proverbs. It is a great way to learn about the Bible and God's Word. The Book of Proverbs makes sense in a very real and practical way.

How did we as a culture get away with falsifying, customizing and misrepresenting the truth for so long? Why has nothing stopped us or prevented us from distorting the truth about any given topic? Here are some possible answers.

Let's start with the topic of money. We spoke earlier of consumerism (mainly for the expanded middle class) as a force that entered into our culture some 50 or 60 years ago. As was the case then and still is now, consumerism has affected a large part of our lives because we spend a fair amount of money and time considering where to go, what to buy, how to entertain ourselves and more. It hasn't taken us long to realize that in today's world we can now have many more things than we could have in years past.

A basic tenet of consumerism is to produce more products and services in order to give people more choices, thereby increasing profits for the manufacturers and retailers. As a consequence, a lot more products and services are continually being made available to us. But we seem never to have understood that *just because something is accessible does not mean that it is acceptable.*

When consumerism began to take hold in our culture and a wider variety of products started to appear in abundance, it challenged the long-established way of thinking (and pathway) that if you do not have the money in your pocket, you cannot afford to buy whatever it is that you want. The old truth was that a person should wait until they have earned enough money to purchase the desired item. That truth changed with the arrival of personal credit. Under the influence of consumerism, you felt you could afford something because someone was willing to lend you the money to buy it. In that sense the truth did evolve. But does that make the "new truth" more correct than the old one? I would say not, or at least not for the average person.

The truth is, that just because someone has access to personal credit, the person is in no better a position to *afford* the purchase. It just so happens that he now has a way to make purchases by borrowing and not because he has worked hard and has earned more money. There is little incentive to discourage these types of transactions, because it would seem that everyone wins here. The manufacturer wins, the store that sells the product wins, the economy wins, the creditor wins, and the consumer gets what he or she wants (along with the debt). Everyone wins, except the truth. It changes, or as we say, it evolves. But more importantly, the notion that the truth can change or evolve as we change, *can itself become a truth*. That means we can look to apply this new truth to all other things in our lives. Therein lies the danger.

There is another factor that helped alter the truth in many areas of life. Simply put, we rarely get caught. For example, you are driving down a local road with a speed limit of 35 MPH. Let's consider that sign to be the established truth. It is part of the law that governs the rules of the road. But how many of us would limit our speed to 35 MPH if a police cruiser was not present? Everybody knows that 35 MPH really means that going 45 MPH or 50 MPH is okay.

Even the police will allow us to exceed speed limits up to a certain point before they pull us over. As a consequence, we have gotten used to substituting our truth (45/50MPH) for the absolute truth, which, in this example, is the posted 35MPH. So in part, because many of us never get caught routinely breaking the law when driving, we feel it is okay to "stretch the truth."

We have become so comfortable with this system that we apply it to virtually all other areas of life. Only after getting caught in a tragic event or major crisis will we consider returning to established safe and proper boundaries or limits. We feel we have the *right* to modify the truth whenever or wherever we feel it is necessary. That is the trump card I spoke of earlier. Unfortunately, the Scriptures are loaded with examples (especially in the Old Testament) of what happens to people who use their trump cards with regard to God's laws. If you do the research you'll find that, in every case, it did not work out well for those who try to trump God's laws.

We should also beware of the "crying wolf syndrome." Remember Y2K? Remember all of the other dire predictions like mankind being wiped out by a nuclear war, asteroids from space, post 9/11 attacks and massive earthquakes on the west coast of our country? These and many other predictions of disaster never seem to amount to anything, or at least have not yet. It seems that the older generations have always warned us about bad consequences when we stray from the truth. Similarly our parents and grandparents also warned us to adhere to the old ways of behaving — going to church, believing in God, and avoiding drugs, for example — or else something bad would happen to us. But since it seems that they were wrong about all of the other dire predictions, our generation felt it could also discount their advice about knowing real truth and values.

This came home to me in a very personal way a few years

ago. I was teaching Sunday school to a group of Catholic school eighth graders one Sunday morning. There were 13 or 14 children in class. One boy was slumped down in his chair with his head down and his arms folded. I knew he was angry about something but I left him alone and hoped he would eventually join the discussion. About halfway through class he suddenly jumped up out of his seat and stood there with his fists clenched at his side. He was visibly shaking and with a near shouting voice he said the following:

*Why do I have to be here?! Why do I have to be here?! No one in my family goes to church. You don't see any of this God stuff on TV, in magazines, books, or online. We don't pray before meals, and my parents and relatives don't talk about God at home. They don't need it at work and I sure don't hear any of my friends talking about God. And besides, it's illegal to talk about this stuff at school! So why do I have to be here??!*

With that outburst, he sat down again and looked even more dejected and unhappy. For him, the truth about God just simply was not in his world. Anything I could tell him about Heaven, Hell, God, and the Scriptures just was not real because he did not see evidence of God anywhere in his daily life experience. Whose fault was that? I am sure that because he did not believe what I was saying about God, he probably would not believe any other type of truth about life that I might try to teach him.

That boy's painful outburst had a profound effect on me. In a few short seconds he encapsulated the truth about how many young folks may really feel about God these days. It is not God's fault that they do not believe in Him; rather it is our fault. Because we do not really believe in Him to the degree that others, such as this young boy, can see Him working in our lives, young people can conclude that, by virtue of our example, He must not exist. This realization made me feel both sad and frightened. I knew then that I had to try to do something about it.

Here's another reason why the truth has become distorted. Many of us older folks feel a deep sense of guilt when we see how our children have grown up. We know down deep that we did not serve them well and, in many cases, we did not teach them the right way to live their lives. In short, we did a very poor job of parenting and teaching them about God. As a consequence, we may feel the need to make up for our past failures by becoming more accommodating to our children and doing more for them as they get older.

We may feel that we should pay more attention to them now than we did in years past. Some of us have tried to become broader-minded, yielding to different points of view and accepting other definitions of the truth especially when discussing matters of faith. As a consequence some of us have gone to great lengths to include and merge other versions of the truth about God into the one we learned as children. We may feel that, to our children, it makes us look more modern, more inclusive, more contemporary and perhaps even more compassionate. But all we might be doing is leading them further from the truth about major life issues.

All of these problems with recognizing the truth tie into a point I made earlier. Many people may feel that the old views and ways of thinking just do not apply to today's issues. So we constantly look for new, fresh ideas to help us. Instead of letting our feelings of guilt drive us back to the God of our childhood and the solid beliefs we grew up with, we allow these new interpretations of the truth to push us further off the right road and away from the real truth. In the process they push us further away from God.

Not too long ago a very good friend of mine and I were talking in general about our culture's belief in God. He summed it up neatly in the following comment:

*Our society is basically made up of three groups of people that have an opinion about God. On the left side of the spectrum we have all of the believers. On the right side we have all of the non-believers. And in the vast middle section of the spectrum, we have all of the make-believers.*

It seems this comment fits in with our discussion of truth. If you were to take a poll of each group in that statement, I am certain that everyone was sure that they had the correct understanding about God and truth. They would feel that their personal beliefs were accurately based in absolute truth concerning God. But of course that cannot be true. Only one of those groups could possibly be correct (if indeed any one group is correct), since their understandings are so diametrically opposed to one another.

The make-believers is the group that intrigues me the most. I can understand the position of the groups on either end of the spectrum, and I respect their thoughts and beliefs, because in order to get to their belief positions, a person would normally have had to give at least some level of thought and study to each of the two positions. It is reasonable to assume that they did their due diligence.

But the folks in the middle probably did not think their viewpoints through to a logical end. They have customized the tenets of their faith to such a point that those ideas might not even qualify as legitimate beliefs. As a result, they could even be referred to as fake Christians. It is easy to spot the discrepancies in peoples' behavior. We call them hypocrites, and young folks today can easily see through their charade.

In the Gospels, Jesus never had a harsh word for anyone he encountered, with the exception of the Pharisees. If you read Matthew 23, you will see Him berating and condemning these teachers of the law because they were *misleading and misguiding the people*. Does that sound familiar? We are considering the need to make U-turns in our lives precisely because many of us are guilty of the same kind of behavior as the Pharisees. When I first entertained this thought, and the possibility that this hypocrisy applied to me and to my actions, it scared the day-lights out of me.

Matthew 23 will also give you an idea as to what kind of behavior bars a person from entrance into Heaven. When we change or alter the truth for our own convenience, then we are in a dangerous place. Furthermore, people think that if they do not say anything to others then they cannot be blamed for misleading them, but those people would be wrong. Even without words we can mislead others. Our conduct, viewed by those around us, speaks volumes. Actions do speak louder than words.

The more prominent a position you hold in your family, work and community, the more people look to you for answers as to how to behave. Our behavior alone could very well be misrepresenting the absolute truths that God himself created. Think about that! We may be guilty of teaching "un-truths" to others regarding His laws or the meaning of His laws simply by the way we live. How great a sin is that in God's eyes?

If we have hurt and misled others in our lives, then we are at risk, just as the Pharisees were. Are you guilty of being a make-believer? If so, have you misled others about the truth in any given issue? Then you need to make a U-turn, plain and simple.

There is a lot more to consider before we actually set out to right some wrongs with a U-turn. First of all we need to be certain that we know what the truth is concerning the issues we want to address with others. If we are going to make a U-turn in our lives we must see where we went wrong in the first place. And that means admitting we were wrong and discovering where we made our errors. Let me give you an example:

If I made a financial mistake in managing my business and the error cost me a small fortune, then before I could take steps to correct my mistake, I should want to find out what basic truths I did not know concerning money management that relate to my case. I would need to go back and relearn whatever truth I missed the first time around. A good way to review what we need to know is to study the actions of some of the great U-turners of all time. They went through the process.

Let's now look at some of these folks who made U-turns and see what we can learn.

*"The tears of faithfulness to your beliefs cleanse your spirit to envision the road ahead. Everything is possible for the person who believes."*

~ Adlin Sinclair;
motivational speaker, humanitarian

# 8

# Some of the Great U-Turners of All Time

*"Example is not the main thing in influencing others. It is the only thing."*

~ Albert Schweitzer (1875-1965);
Recipient of the 1952 Nobel Peace Prize

John Newton is the man credited with writing the song Amazing Grace, a favorite among Christians of all denominations. I am sure it has positively affected people of other faiths as well. Few of us know that John Newton was a slave trader by profession. His childhood was anything but easy, losing his mother to illness when he was seven years of age. His father, a merchant sailor brought him to sea at the age of 11. He was abducted and pressed into service on a British man-of-war ship seven years later.

He eventually became first mate on a ship that took part in the lucrative business of slave trading. The traders would leave England with essentially an empty ship, drop anchor off the coast of Africa and trade with various tribes for war prisoners caught from other tribes. The slaves would be chained in the hold of the ship, lying side by side. As many as 600 slaves per trip might be crammed in and stowed on the ship. The living conditions were so horrible that the slaves were kept away from the upper decks of the ship for fear that they would commit suicide. It was in the slave traders' interests to keep as many of the captives alive and in reasonably good health as possible during the trip. That would insure a profit from the journey.

With this as a backdrop to the story, we can see the kind of man John Newton was and the kind of brutal work he engaged in prior to his conversion. On the homeward leg of one of his voyages, his ship and crew encountered a violent storm and the ship began taking on water. He recorded in his journal that he thought all was lost, so he appealed to God out of sheer desperation. It has been said that he spoke the words "Lord, have mercy upon us." Once out of danger, he thought about what had transpired and believed that God had spoken to him through the storm. He felt that God's grace had saved him.

John Newton was a great U-turner. His motivation for the U-turn may have been made out of desperation, but it was a U-turn nonetheless. And what is even more important, he stuck to his promise to stay with the Lord. For the rest of his life he observed the anniversary of May 10, 1748 as the day of his conversion, a day when he subjected his will to a higher power. Records show that the original version of the song contained the following verses:

*Amazing grace! (how sweet the sound)*
*That sav'd a wretch like me!*
*I once was lost, but now am found,*
*Was blind, but now I see.*

*'Twas grace that taught my heart to fear,*
*And grace my fears reliev'd;*
*How precious did that grace appear,*
*The hour I first believ'd!*

*Thro' many dangers, toils and snares,*
*I have already come;*
*'Tis grace has brought me safe thus far,*
*And grace will lead me home.*

*The Lord has promis'd good to me,*
*His word my hope secures;*
*He will my shield and portion be,*
*As long as life endures.*

*Yes, when this flesh and heart shall fail,*
*And mortal life shall cease;*
*I shall possess, within the veil,*
*A life of joy and peace.*

*The earth shall soon dissolve like snow,*
*The sun forbear to shine;*
*But God, who call'd me here below,*
*Will be forever mine.*

I just love to read and drink in the meaning of the words. Even without the music their powerful meaning has had the same effect on many generations of people as they had on the composer. You can almost feel how they were born onto the paper as John Newton was first composing the song. The Lord can work through any situation regardless of how lost we may feel or how far off course we may be at the time.

The character Ebenezer Scrooge represents a man who could have lived anywhere in the world at any time. *A Christmas Carol* was written by Charles Dickens in 1843, and tells the story of Scrooge, an elderly man who, while becoming wealthy also had become cynical and bitter in his life. As a consequence, he reflected those attitudes on everyone he encountered. Through a series of visits from three ghosts over the course of a Christmas Eve, he begins to realize what he has done with his life. Even though he suffered through a tough childhood, Scrooge sees all of the opportunities he had lost and how he allowed relationships with precious people and chances for happiness to pass him by.

As the story progresses, Dickens does a good job of evoking the reader's sense of dislike and eventual pity for the man. However, I could also relate to the character of Scrooge on a personal level since many of the traits that he displays are very human and common to us all. I think the story is written purposely so as to create sympathy for Scrooge but also to get readers to see some of the very same traits in themselves. Scrooges' failings are not unlike our own.

The pivotal moment in the story comes when Scrooge awakens on Christmas morning to find that he still has time to right some of the wrongs in his life. He still has time to make that U-turn he needs so desperately. We can appreciate the joy he experiences, as well as the happiness of all of his contemporaries, when he decides to turn his life around. The effect of the U-turn is amazing. It touches the whole community and makes believers of many people. If God can touch as hard a soul as Scrooge, He can reach anyone. The message we receive is that there is hope for us all and that it is never too late to change.

But why wait? Why run the risk of losing the precious moments you need to make the U-turn and the subsequent time you need to right wrongs you have committed? The message is clear: make your U-turn now. Wait no longer; *do it now*.

You may remember the story of the two criminals that were being crucified along with Christ.

*Two other men, both criminals, were also led out with him to be executed. When they came to the place called the Skull, there they crucified him, along with the criminals — one on his right, the other on his left. Jesus said, "Father, forgive them, for they do not know what they are doing." And they divided up his clothes by casting lots.*

*The people stood watching, and the rulers even sneered at him. They said, "He saved others; let him save himself if he is the Christ of God, the Chosen One."*

*The soldiers also came up and mocked him. They offered him wine vinegar and said, "If you are the king of the Jews, save yourself."*

*There was a written notice above him, which read: THIS IS THE KING OF THE JEWS.*

*One of the criminals who hung there hurled insults at him: "Aren't you the Christ? Save yourself and us!"*

*But the other criminal rebuked him. "Don't you fear God," he said, "since you are under the same sentence? We are punished justly, for we are getting what our deeds deserve. But this man has done nothing wrong."*

*Then he said, "Jesus, remember me when you come into your kingdom."*

*Jesus answered him, "I tell you the truth, today you will be with me in paradise."* (Luke 23:32-43)

The second criminal decided to make his U-turn at virtually the last moment of his life. I would not advise waiting that long, for you never know how quickly the end may come upon you. But in this man's case, it shows how anxious Christ is to accept lost sheep back into His fold. There is great hope for us all even up to the very last moment of life as we know it. This passage also demonstrates how God will deal with us on that last day. He will not force any of us to accept Him. He will not impose Himself on us and not require us to go to Heaven. Plain and simple, if we are to end up in Heaven, it will be because we want to be there with Him and we will have made that choice while in this life.

Then there is the Biblical case of the tax collector known as Zacchaeus:

> *Jesus entered Jericho and was passing through. A man was there by the name of Zacchaeus; he was a chief tax collector and was wealthy. He wanted to see who Jesus was, but being a short man he could not, because of the crowd. So he ran ahead and climbed a sycamore-fig tree to see him, since Jesus was coming that way.*
> *When Jesus reached the spot, he looked up and said to him, "Zacchaeus, come down immediately. I must stay at your house today." So he came down at once and welcomed him gladly.*
> *All the people saw this and began to mutter, "He has gone to be the guest of a 'sinner.'"*
> *But Zacchaeus stood up and said to the Lord, "Look, Lord! Here and now I give half of my possessions to the poor, and if I have cheated anybody out of anything, I will pay back four times the amount."*
> *Jesus said to him, "Today salvation has come to this house, because this man, too, is a son of Abraham. For the Son of Man came to seek and to save what was lost."*

(Luke 19:1-10)

Zacchaeus was a notorious tax collector in the eyes of many residents. Tax collectors had the reputation of being cheats who often gouged the people. As a group they were hated, and they were seen as great sinners especially by the Jewish population of the day. Jesus, in this case, approached the man directly, and by the sheer force of His spirit Zacchaeus responded favorably to Christ.

Here is another case of a U-turner that did not take a great deal of convincing to turn his life around. If we use this story as a model for ourselves, we can see that in God's eyes it does not take much for us to qualify as potential U-turners. All we have to do is recognize that we are wrong in how we are living and proclaim that we will change our heading 180 degrees. Of course we will have to follow through with our claim by taking the appropriate actions.

Also, look at how Christ responded to the tax collector. He proclaims that salvation is the reward for following Him. By promising to make a U-turn, Zacchaeus would now enjoy the benefits of eternal life. Not a bad deal at all. You may have noticed that Zacchaeus received the same response that the thief on the cross received when he asked Christ for forgiveness. It was a quick, deliberate, open-armed acceptance by Jesus. In the following verses, we will see how important repentance is to God.

*Then Jesus told them this parable: "Suppose one of you has a hundred sheep and loses one of them. Does he not leave the ninety-nine in the open country and go after the lost sheep until he finds it? And when he finds it, he joyfully puts it on his shoulders and goes home. Then he calls his friends and neighbors together and says, 'Rejoice*

*with me; I have found my lost sheep.' I tell you that in*
*the same way there will be more rejoicing in heaven*
*over one sinner who repents than over ninety-nine*
*righteous persons who do not need to repent. "*

(Luke 15:3-7 emphasis added)

So how important is making a U-turn in our lives? Judging from the above verses, nothing is *more* important. If all of Heaven is rejoicing each time someone repents, that should give us an even better appreciation of its importance.

Matthew, one of the Gospel writers, was also first employed as a tax collector. Jesus recruited him as well. It is said that Matthew just got up and started to follow Christ even as he was in the midst of collecting taxes one day. In essence, that's like coming to a screeching halt and whipping your car around in order to complete the U-turn as quickly as possible. Matthew wasted no time in complying with Christ's call (see Matthew 9:9).

If we are going to discuss repentance and making U-turns, we cannot avoid the Parable of the Prodigal Son, perhaps the undisputed king of all U-turners in all of history! I believe it is the most pivotal and critical story that Christ told. Let's review what the Scriptures tell us.

*There was a man who had two sons. The younger one*
*said to his father, "Father, give me my share of the*
*estate." So he divided his property between them.*
*Not long after that, the younger son got together all he*
*had, set off for a distant country and there squandered*
*his wealth in wild living. After he had spent*
*everything, there was a severe famine in that whole*

132

*country, and he began to be in need. So he went and hired himself out to a citizen of that country, who sent him to his fields to feed pigs. He longed to fill his stomach with the pods that the pigs were eating, but no one gave him anything.*

*When he came to his senses, he said, "How many of my father's hired men have food to spare, and here I am starving to death! I will set out and go back to my father and say to him: Father, I have sinned against heaven and against you. I am no longer worthy to be called your son; make me like one of your hired men." So he got up and went to his father.*

*But while he was still a long way off, his father saw him and was filled with compassion for him; he ran to his son, threw his arms around him and kissed him.*

*The son said to him, "Father, I have sinned against heaven and against you. I am no longer worthy to be called your son."*

*But the father said to his servants, "Quick! Bring the best robe and put it on him. Put a ring on his finger and sandals on his feet. Bring the fattened calf and kill it. Let's have a feast and celebrate. For this son of mine was dead and is alive again; he was lost and is found." So they began to celebrate.*

*Meanwhile, the older son was in the field. When he came near the house, he heard music and dancing. So he called one of the servants and asked him what was going on. "Your brother has come," he replied, "and your father has killed the fattened calf because he has him back safe and sound."*

*The older brother became angry and refused to go in. So*

*his father went out and pleaded with him. But he*
*answered his father, "Look! All these years I've been*
*slaving for you and never disobeyed your orders. Yet you*
*never gave me even a young goat so I could celebrate*
*with my friends. But when this son of yours who has*
*squandered your property with prostitutes comes home,*
*you kill the fattened calf for him!"*
*"My son," the father said, "you are always with me, and*
*everything I have is yours. But we had to celebrate and*
*be glad, because this brother of yours was dead and is*
*alive again; he was lost and is found."*     (Luke 15:11-32)

So much that happens in this story relates to us today. The younger son prematurely asks his father for his inheritance while his father is still alive. This was a great insult to his father, but the son did not care. His desire was to be "free" from his father's rule and control. He wished to have things his own way while making his way through his life. Interestingly, the father does not argue or reprimand or even try to dissuade his son. He simply grants him his wish and allows him to leave.

Is that not what God does with each of us even today? He knows that what we frequently want and ask for is wrong. But we have free will, which allows us to choose what we want and He allows that free will to have its way with us. How many times in the past have we insulted those who love us and who want nothing more than what is best for us? And still, we insist on having our own way.

The younger son goes away, the Scriptures tell us, to indulge himself in all kinds of pleasures. This sounds all too familiar, does it not? How many people in our Boomer generation have done this very thing over the last 40 or 50 years? The son finally "hits the wall" in the form of a severe famine. Now he has spent all of his money and everything else that he had, and is in great need. As the saying goes, "what goes around comes around."

The son, however, has enough presence of mind to realize what he must do. He realizes that he needs to repent. He needs to go home to his father, apologize to him and do what he can to repair the relationship and take care of whatever else that needs his attention. The son was so hungry that what was feed for the pigs was beginning to appeal to him. In a sense, he was staring into the pig trough of his life when he suddenly came to his senses. In our terms, he needed to make a U-turn and he was smart enough to take the opportunity to do it.

And that is the core message of this book and my reason for writing it. Many of us either are approaching or are already at the same point as the younger son in the story. Will we come to our senses in time? Will we finally decide to do what it takes to make things right with God and those in our lives? The timing is perfect. Many of us are thinking of retirement and enjoying ourselves when there is so much that needs to be done and corrected, from both the past and the present.

Much fault may be heaped on the Prodigal Son, but the fact is, he repented. He did the right thing and was rewarded for it. He came through in the end. Will your story have a similar ending? *Remember, how you started is not as important as how you finish.*

Consider the father in the story. He let his son go to do his thing. He must have known what the son was up to, but still he did not deny his request. (As I said, God does that with us.) He did not chase after the son even when it was apparent he would not be returning soon, if ever. However, the father kept watch for him. He was constantly scanning the horizon in the hope that he would return. When he did return, the son can barely form an apology before his dad began heaping rewards on him. That is exactly what God is anxious to do with us. He is allowing us to have and use our free will and He is anxiously waiting for us to return.

Do not miss this critical point: in the story, the father's joy is boundless, because, as he says, *"For this son of mine was dead and is alive again; he was lost and is found."*

The son was lost while he was away from his father. He was dead and lost. Most of us do not realize what that means: Jesus was (and still is) telling us that nothing less than our eternal salvation is at stake here. While we remain apart from God, all is lost. If we choose to take the road filled with sinful behavior, then we choose to be forever separate from God.

As it was with the Prodigal Son, our Father will honor our choices. These decisions affect our eternal salvation. God will never force anyone into Heaven or into Hell. Our choices do that for us. The father made this point twice in the story; once to all of his servants and again to the older son. Make no mistake; when he left his dad, the Prodigal Son was playing with fire... eternal fire.

However, this is where the story gets very interesting. The older son learns of his brother's return and that the father is giving a party in his honor. The older son protests that he has worked all his life for his father and has given all that he had in service to the family. He is angry and jealous of his younger brother and feels that he should be the one receiving the praise and reward. The story ends with the father practically begging his older son to come into the party. But the son refuses and it seems that, as the story ends, he chooses instead to remain away from the party and his family.

He now becomes the lost son by virtue of his jealousy and sin. It seems that all the while the older son was harboring ill will toward his brother who squandered the father's wealth with prostitutes. He resented his father for never giving him a party or any reward, as well as for granting the younger son's request for his inheritance.

Thus, we have another thought to ponder. Why did the older brother not go after his younger brother or try to dissuade him from taking that trip to begin with? The story does not tell us and, in all fairness, we may imagine him having a few words with him before he left. But we realize at the end of the story how the older son really felt about his brother and father. We must question who is the lost son in the end? Again, how you start is not as important as how you finish.

How many of us fit the description of the older son? Like him, we have been very dutiful in giving money and time to support our church and going to services each week. We try to be good people and good Christians. We want to be known as the "good sons and daughters." We sometimes wonder what we have to show for it. Is that how you feel? The father said something else that is very important: he told the older son that while he was with the father he had all that the father had. In other words, he was safe in the father's love, he was not lost and dead. It appears that the older son rejected this and did not appreciate his father. We need to ask ourselves if we have ever acted that way with God?

So who, in fact, turns out to be the lost son in the story? The younger son was dead and lost but came back and was found again (see "Amazing Grace"). He was saved. The older son seemed to be safe all along but his heart was far from the father. He turns out to be the lost soul. In the end he has to choose which way to go, but, sadly, it seems his anger and hatred will cost him everything.

If you were to be honest with yourself, which son would you say you most resemble? Furthermore, which one would you rather be?

Finally, let's look into the story of a beggar named Lazarus. This Lazarus is not the same Lazarus whom Christ raised from the dead (see John 11:1). This is the story of a rich man who terribly regrets not making a U-turn when he had the chance.

*There was a rich man who was dressed in purple and fine linen and lived in luxury every day. At his gate was laid a beggar named Lazarus, covered with sores and longing to eat what fell from the rich man's table. Even the dogs came and licked his sores.*

*The time came when the beggar died and the angels carried him to Abraham's side. The rich man also died and was buried. In hell, where he was in torment, he looked up and saw Abraham far away, with Lazarus by his side. So he called to him, "Father Abraham, have pity on me and send Lazarus to dip the tip of his finger in water and cool my tongue, because I am in agony in this fire."*

*But Abraham replied, "Son, remember that in your lifetime you received your good things, while Lazarus received bad things, but now he is comforted here and you are in agony. And besides all this, between us and you a great chasm has been fixed, so that those who want to go from here to you cannot, nor can anyone cross over from there to us."*

*He answered, "Then I beg you, father, send Lazarus to my father's house, for I have five brothers. Let him*

*warn them, so that they will not also come to this place*
*of torment."*
*Abraham replied, "They have Moses and the Prophets;*
*let them listen to them."*
*"No, father Abraham," he said, "but if someone from the*
*dead goes to them, they will repent."*
*He said to him, "If they do not listen to Moses and the*
*Prophets, they will not be convinced even if someone*
*rises from the dead."*                              (Luke 16:19-31)

Here is another seldom-heard story straight from the mouth of Christ. This illustrates one of those "inconvenient truths" that Jesus spoke about in His ministry. Many people resist the notion that there may be a place of eternal torment reserved for some of us after we die. But this quote is clear and does not leave any room for alternate interpretations.

It simply tells us that there will come a time of great sorrow for those of us who do not repent. Some of us (perhaps many) who have chosen not to make that U-turn in life when they had the chance will severely regret their decision. To say it will be a sad moment is the understatement of the millennium.

Making a U-turn is serious business. It affects so much and so many, not only in this life but in the next as well. Before we discuss the details of how to make a successful U-turn, we need to talk about the "old paths" that are mentioned in Jeremiah:

*This is what the LORD says:*
*Stand at the crossroads and look;*
*ask for the ancient paths,*
*ask where the good way is, and walk in it,*
*and you will find rest for your souls.*          (Jeremiah 6:16)

Think about this. When we find ourselves lost in unfamiliar surroundings, we always look for something that is familiar, something that we will recognize and will help us find our way home. When people go off on a journey to another town, city, or country, they follow the established routes and paths, since they usually are the best and most travelled roads. The travellers know that if they follow those paths they will know where they are at all times and they will arrive safely at their destination.

With regard to best practices in life, I think that you can simply examine the stories in this chapter and judge for yourself what the best responses and reactions were in each case. Simply extend the proper response to your own situation. It would be difficult for me to imagine a situation where repenting for something we did wrong could ever be the wrong thing to do.

If we are going to make a U-turn in our lives, however, we will be heading into what might be uncharted territory. In essence we will be looking for the right path and way to travel. I realize that many of us have never tried this before. We will need to keep our bearings about us. We will need to prepare for this task and know the truth about how best to accomplish the results we seek. So it makes sense that we take some time to study what exactly are the ancient paths and the good ways that Jeremiah speaks of and that is the topic of our next chapter.

*"When one man, for whatever reason, has the opportunity to lead an extraordinary life, he has no right to keep it to himself."*

~ Jacques Cousteau (1910-1997);
marine biologist, diver, explorer

# 9

## The Old Paths and the Good Way

*"If a man does not know what port he is steering for, no wind is favorable to him."*

~Seneca (4-65);
philosopher

Putting this chapter together has proven to be very difficult. If you had to suggest, in relatively short terms, the most important, dependable, and reliable ways of living, which choices would you offer? Where would you go to find them? What resources would you use? As one would imagine, there are many opinions and many places to look for the answers. When I asked myself these questions, I opted for the supernatural source of information. I once again decided to turn to the Scriptures.

Let's take a look at another part of Jeremiah 6:16, as well as some other relevant passages concerning the old paths.

> *This is what the LORD says:*
> *"Stand at the crossroads and look;*
> *ask for the ancient* [eternal] *paths,*
> *ask where the good way is, and walk in it,*
> *and you will find rest for your souls.*
> *But you said, 'We will not walk in it.'*
> *I appointed watchmen over you and said,*

*'listen to the sound of the trumpet!'*
*But you said, 'We will not listen.'"*

(Jeremiah 6:16-17, note added)

Earlier on in this book, I suggested that we should utilize the theory of best practices when considering the best way to live a successful and rewarding life. This is a good place to apply that concept in order to answer our questions. The Scriptures are a timeless resource. If you think about it, we are getting the best of both worlds in Scripture. Since the Bible is inspired by God we know that we are receiving the absolute truth, and since it is written by man, we know that it will be expressed in real-life terms we can all understand. It will be practical advice that we can follow no matter how many years have passed since the words were first penned. They do, in fact, provide us with a very dependable source of best practices. History has proven that point.

The "ancient paths" referred to in Jeremiah 6:16 actually translate to "eternal" paths. If we look for those paths and ways of living in this present life, we will not only find the kingdom of God here on earth, but the pathway will continue on and ultimately lead us to the next life. And since eternal life is our ultimate destination, how imperative is it for us to find these old paths here and now? In this sense, the old paths have serious eternal implications for each of us. Consider another reference to this topic:

*Enter through the narrow gate. For wide is the gate and broad is the road that leads to destruction, and many enter through it. But small is the gate and narrow the road that leads to life, and only a few find it.*

(Matthew 7:13-14)

142

The paths that lead to eternal life are not necessarily well marked, even though they are old and so well established. Quite a few people from generation to generation have accessed these pathways and have found peace and well-being. However, in relative terms, it's possible that the vast majority of people who have lived through the ages have not taken advantage of them. I can say this with some degree of certainty, because these pathways are not legibly marked and have not been well maintained. They are hard to find despite their age. We can clearly see that this is especially true in our modern-day culture.

It is the broad way that is usually taken these days because it is so convenient, with fewer obstacles for those walking along it. But the question remains; where is the broad way ultimately taking us? Scripture tells us that taking the narrower roads and more challenging paths will lead us to where we really should be going. In a more familiar expression, they are the roads less travelled.

Ever since we crossed over into the 21st century, popular thinking has argued that the future, and not the past, holds the keys to our success and happiness. Many believe that our technological advances and contemporary theories pertaining to life and spirituality have proven that the truth is ever evolving and eluding our grasp. Our job, one supposes, is to catch up to the truth and possess it before it changes and moves off again, perhaps in a different direction.

But in reality, just the opposite is true. The old paths and the ancient ways of living and believing contain the eternal truths. Think about it. How arrogant would we be to think that we are the first ones in all of human history to discover the truth about life and correct living? Those who have come before us, even many centuries before us, have already discovered the truth.

When we discus the truth about life and moral beliefs with others, we have to remember that everything that is really important about life is already known. It is up to us to rediscover it and re-apply it to our lives. This has been the case for many generations before ours; to live successfully, we have to go back and relearn the old ways and paths in order to move forward. In other words, we must make a U-turn; we must go back in order to go forward.

As I write these words, our national economy is in the midst of a great recession which is resulting in significant financial and emotional stress in the lives of many people. Many are unemployed and suffering. Economists tell us that the recession is over even though many are still out of work. We are threatened with the possibility of another recession or even a depression. We are indeed weary and burdened but who will we turn to? If the Scriptures presented above are a good forecaster of human behavior, then they predict that we will not turn to God. We will not go back to Him. We will wait until we have lost everything, perhaps like the Prodigal Son, and then, maybe, we will try to return. At that point will we have the opportunity and time to do so? Do we really want to take that chance and wait that long?

In the passages above, Jeremiah said that the Lord exhorts us to find the old and trusted, time-worn paths. He says to stand at the crossroads and look for the dependable and time-tested ways of living. Many in today's society are taking the broad and easy road to travel on their way. It seems fewer and fewer people even are aware of the old paths. The Lord instructs us to ask others where those paths are located. In many cases, the paths will be hard to find because so few people access them these days.

We are told to be careful, however, and not just follow the

crowds. It is very critical that we find the right road. The clear meaning from Scripture is that there are *not* many different ways to live successfully in God's eyes. His rules and expectations are quite definitive. Not all ways of living please Him and not all paths lead to Him; if they did, then why would we need the Bible, clergy, or churches of any faith? Let's put aside God and the Scriptures for a moment and ask whether we as Baby Boomers discovered different paths to truly successful living? If so what are they? Can they be named and modeled for others to see and copy? If these paths exist, who would lead us along the way? Would it be Jesus, or someone else?

Very predictably, most people will not follow the old paths. They are difficult to traverse, and they seem old and outdated. The new version of most anything these days is sought after more than the old one. We refer to the old version of things with terms such as vintage or retro, and we look at them as obsolete novelties and try to imagine how people could have made do with them.

In a way, many of us feel that the beliefs and behaviors of an older generation are simply ignorant of our more modern and successful ways of living. It is inconceivable to some of us that the older generations could have known so much of the truth concerning life. We fail to see how they could be of help to those of us alive today.

We live in an age of modern communication and transportation. Instant cash, instant food, instant credit, instant marriage, instant sex, along with any number of other things we have always wanted are constantly available. Obviously, our excesses have surpassed those of our ancestors by great leaps and bounds. It is therefore assumed that our knowledge concerning the really important things in life has improved and advanced as well. If this is true, then what modern paths exist that could substitute for those which Jeremiah speaks of? These modern paths should be obvious to us by now, shouldn't they?

To add to our modern spoils, we have also made God into essentially a God of love, tolerance and peace. One of the core tenets of our practical-based theology today is that humans are basically good and that we all need to have more patience with one another. We should tolerate others, especially those with whom we do not agree. We should give them more of a chance to "come around" to our way of thinking. And if they do not, then we should adapt and work with them. After all, we have come to believe that there are many paths to God these days, are there not?

We reason that our higher level of learning and living has taught all of us that the right path includes tolerance and acceptance of other paths and alternate routes. We have crossed into the 21st century, we are advancing and we are leaving many of the old outdated ways behind us. We are making progress! But the big question now before us is: will we also leave the words of Scripture behind? God represents an old way of thinking and living. Does progress mean that we can leave God behind?

For many of us the answer must be a resounding no. Yet, as some of us search for more modern paths on the road to successful living, we have developed the idea of taking God along with us and *making Him into the kind of God we need.* Apparently, we now have that power. If you doubt what I say, just look at the polling done by groups such as Pew Research and the Barna Group regarding our moral behavior and spiritual beliefs, especially among younger people. The Barna Group issued a very telling report on this topic on 12/13/10 entitled "Six Megathemes Emerge from Barna Group Research in 2010."

Mainline Christian churches are growing smaller by the day. Many young people find religion, for the most part, to be irrelevant. Still, we are not quite ready to go it alone without God. We can solve the dilemma in the following manner: *we* no longer become born again. In the 21st century it is *God* who must be born again, each person remaking Him into the kind of god they want and need. That way He becomes a more user-friendly God. We'll take Him along with us into the 21st century and He will evolve as we evolve. If you think about it, this is how many of us live. Remember, our generation was raised to be consumers. Our entire Baby Boomer generation thrives on consumption and having things virtually custom-made to meet our specific needs. So, God, in a way, has become a commodity. He can be custom-redesigned and re-built to meet our personal needs. Remember the old Burger King slogan "Have it your way?" The good news for us is that we can now have God our way!

The error in fashioning God to our liking reminds me of the story of the golden calf during the time of Moses. The Israelites gave up on God and designed an idol, a golden statue of a calf. It did not work out very well for them. Read Exodus, chapter 32. Many people have never read those verses. I only had to read them once, and once was enough. I think you will be shocked to see how God reacted and what happened to the Israelites.

So, shall we go back and look for the old paths or look for new ones? If you look in the Old Testament, as well as in many other secular sources that describe the "old days" in history, you will find families working hard at transferring knowledge and truth to their children. Stories about certain family members are passed on from generation to generation. Why is this? Because those past experiences contained real truth and that truth was too precious to lose. We trusted those who loved and lived with us.

The stories that were passed down contained truth even when the facts surrounding the events may have been changed or lost in translation (similar in tone and theme to the stories in the Bible). But the messages contained in each of the Bible stories are 100% truthful. We can believe in them since they came directly from God. We can believe them because we believe He loves us more than anything.

The first old pathway to speak of is the most important one of all: the old habit of reading the Scriptures every day, not only for our own edification, but also for our families and friends. I know of some well-educated people who will not even begin to read the verses found in the Bible. They can't imagine that such old words and ways of speaking could be valuable or relevant to us today. They cannot fathom that these words could eventually lead them to a place like Heaven.

Look at how Charles Spurgeon describes it in *Morning and Evening: Daily Readings by Charles Haddon Spurgeon*:

*"The hope which is laid up for you in heaven."*
*Colossians 1:5*

"Our hope in Christ for the future is the mainspring and the mainstay of our joy here. It will animate our hearts to think often of heaven, for all that we can desire is promised there. Here we are weary and toil worn, but yonder is the land of *rest* where the sweat of labor shall no more bedew the worker's brow, and fatigue shall be for ever banished. To those who are weary and spent, the word 'rest' is full of heaven. We are always in the field of battle; we are so tempted within, and so molested by foes without, that we have little or no peace; but in heaven we shall enjoy the *victory,* when the banner shall be waved aloft in triumph, and the sword shall be sheathed, and we shall hear our Captain say, 'Well done, good and faithful servant.' We have suffered bereavement after bereavement, but we are going to the land of the *immortal* where graves are unknown things. Here sin is a constant grief to us, but there we shall be perfectly *holy,* for there shall by no means enter into that kingdom anything which defileth. Hemlock springs not up in the furrows of celestial fields. Oh! is it not joy that you are not to be in banishment for ever, that you are not to dwell eternally in this wilderness, but shall soon inherit Canaan? Nevertheless let it never be said of us, that we are dreaming about the *future* and forgetting the *present,* let the future sanctify the present to highest uses. Through the Spirit of God the hope of heaven is the most potent force for the product of virtue; it is a fountain of joyous effort, it is the corner stone of cheerful holiness. The man who has this hope in him goes about his work with vigor, for the joy of the Lord is his strength. He fights against temptation with ardor, for the hope of the next world repels the fiery darts of the adversary. He can labor without present reward, for he looks for a reward in the world to come."

Once we agree that getting back to the Bible on a daily basis is one of the correct paths to be on, then lots of other "old paths" start to emerge. Following the Ten Commandments, for example, seems to be a prudent course of action. Worshipping God alone, keeping holy the Sabbath, not using God's name or personage in a bad way, honoring our parents and elders, refraining from killing, stealing, adultery, etc all come into view as old pathways.

We may think that we are not personally guilty of breaking

these laws and that therefore we are safe. The fact remains, however, that we are guilty of allowing our culture to grow in such a way that it glorifies breaking many of these old laws. We may have never committed actual adultery but we might have indulged in the next best thing, which is lustful fantasizing.

Perhaps we stood by as others talked about their sexual conquests and other immoral behavior but said nothing to set them straight. The old paths are indeed very difficult to travel.

The paths we are speaking of were set down by God Himself long ago. I spoke of the "fencing" analogy in an earlier chapter. This is exactly what I was trying to explain. Those old pathways and guide lanes that our elders built for us have existed since ancient times. They represent a distillation of the best of the best practices that people have passed along. We discarded a great deal of those practices in the latter half of the 20th century, and now we are paying for it. How? In many different ways, but one, in particular, stands out: we have no rest for our souls. We are all running faster than ever before. We are tired, exhausted and seem to have no clue where we are going. And what's worse, many of us feel in our "collective gut" that we are headed in the wrong direction.

Going further with this observation, quite a few of us these days have been pursuing one of the newest paths available, the "work-to-play path." We continue to knock ourselves out day in and day out, anticipating the next vacation, pay raise, golf date, or some other temporary pleasure or event. The end game for those of us on this path is the same: a box in the ground somewhere, probably at a premature point in our lives.

*Come to me, all you who are weary and burdened, and I will give you rest. Take my yoke upon you and learn from me, for I am gentle and humble in heart, and you will find rest for your souls. For my yoke is easy and my burden is light.*      (Matthew 11:28-30)

We have little or no peace and want to know where we can find it. We will find it along the pathway described in Matthew 11:28. Jesus clearly has that one covered for us. But will we seek that from Him? Probably not, or at least most of us will not, unless something major threatens us and we have enough time to respond.

One particularly important old pathway that I remember from my youth was Sunday, the day of rest. It was set aside mainly for focusing on church and family. I don't think many of us realized how much we needed that "down time," so we could step back from our work routine and enjoy quiet moments with God and family. That is what we need as a society. Setting aside the day of rest would be the second old path I would re-establish, after daily Scripture reading.

Speaking of old paths, we could closely read all four gospels in their entirety, tracing the steps of Christ from one event to another, and that would also give us a great path to follow. Jesus did it for us. He set up the model that we could follow. As a matter of fact, the people who were with Him when He died followed that model.

After Jesus was gone His followers were utterly devastated. So what did they do? Did they give up? No, they did not. Instead they took to heart the lessons they learned from watching and listening to Him. They recognized the old paths because they saw Jesus walking along them and talking constantly of them. They continued along those paths, adopting them for their own. The "Early Christian Church" was thus formed, and it flourished despite persecution and troubles.

Interestingly, the early church was not known as that in its very early days. The followers of Christ were known as those who walk along "the Way," or "followers of the Way." So the concept of being on the right road was with us from the very beginning.

This is an important point. The path Jesus took was one of yielding to His Father. He gave Himself up for our sake. How many times do we see Him repeat this in His ministry years? He yielded to the wishes of His father even in the Garden at Gethsemane. As He said to His father, *"...yet not my will, but yours be done"* (Luke 22:42). That is the key for us in this discussion. We have to yield to God the trump card we hold in the form of our free will. Yielding our will to God's is an old path that few seem anxious to follow today.

As I mentioned earlier, not long ago there was a phrase circulating among the Christian community that asked, "What would Jesus do?" This precept is a good place for someone to start in following Christ. But it leaves us with too much room for speculation. A better question is "What *did* Jesus do?" Such a question requires research in the Gospels, another essential path to follow, as I mentioned earlier. We must do what Jesus did even though He had the advantage of being God.

There are other extremely vital pathways to follow, such as those for worshipping God the Father, loving God the Father and loving one another. Confession, too, is a very old pathway, one that God speaks of even in the first book of the Bible, Genesis. It is an important path we should use whenever we know we have sinned against Him or against one another.

Being in constant contact with God will help us as we seek out these pathways. While these are ancient roads for sure, they are all good for us to follow because they lead us to Christ and they keep us close to Him. As Saint Augustine said, "*Our souls can find no rest until they rest in Thee.*"

Another source for those seeking the old paths may be found in hymns. If you go back and listen to old recordings, or even some of the new songs whose lyrics are faithful to Christian core concepts, you will find guidance in song. Give me that old time religion, as the song goes.

For example, look at the lyrics in the song "How Great Thou Art:"

> *O Lord my God, When I in awesome wonder,*
> *Consider all the worlds Thy Hands have made;*
> *I see the stars, I hear the rolling thunder,*
> *Thy power throughout the universe displayed.*

> *Then sings my soul, My Saviour God, to Thee,*
> *How great Thou art, How great Thou art.*
> *Then sings my soul, My Saviour God, to Thee,*
> *How great Thou art, How great Thou art!*

> *When through the woods, and forest glades I wander,*
> *And hear the birds sing sweetly in the trees.*
> *When I look down, from lofty mountain grandeur*
> *And see the brook, and feel the gentle breeze.*

> *Then sings my soul, My Saviour God, to Thee,*
> *How great Thou art, How great Thou art.*
> *Then sings my soul, My Saviour God, to Thee,*
> *How great Thou art, How great Thou art!*

*And when I think, that God, His Son not sparing;*
*Sent Him to die, I scarce can take it in;*
*That on the Cross, my burden gladly bearing,*
*He bled and died to take away my sin.*

*Then sings my soul, My Saviour God, to Thee,*
*How great Thou art, How great Thou art.*
*Then sings my soul, My Saviour God, to Thee,*
*How great Thou art, How great Thou art!*

*When Christ shall come, with shout of acclamation,*
*And take me home, what joy shall fill my heart.*
*Then I shall bow, in humble adoration,*
*And then proclaim: "My God, how great Thou art!"*

*Then sings my soul, My Saviour God, to Thee,*
*How great Thou art, How great Thou art.*
*Then sings my soul, My Saviour God, to Thee,*
*How great Thou art, How great Thou art!"*

Wikipedia describes the origins of this song as follows:

*"How Great Thou Art" is a Christian hymn based on a Swedish poem written by Carl Gustav Boberg (1859–1940) in Sweden in 1885. The melody is a Swedish folk song. It was translated into English by British missionary Stuart K. Hine, who also added two original verses of his own composition. It was popularized by George Beverly Shea and Cliff Barrows during Billy Graham crusades. It was voted the United Kingdom's favorite hymn by BBC's Songs of Praise. "How Great Thou Art" was ranked second (after*

*"Amazing Grace") on a list of the favorite hymns of all time in a survey by* Today's Christian *magazine in 2001.*

In just one hymn, we can hear the heart of the Christian story, and gain a clear view of the old paths. The composers of the old hymns, in my view, were as inspired by God as were the authors of the words in the Bible. They knew the way home and wrote about it in song.

Finally, let's not forget that Jeremiah tells us to not only *find* the good ways but also *to walk in them.* Nothing is more important than that. We can study the Bible all we want but if we do not walk along the right paths, our effort is for nothing. I have been present at many Bible studies, retreats and Christian conferences over the years and many of those in attendance have lacked that final piece... *walking the talk.*

I sometimes think that while many of us are well-meaning Christians, we are like a group of very overweight people who decide to try to lose weight. We get together each week to study various new diet plans. Week after week we arrive at the meeting with all the new and available diet plans that we find. We discuss them in great detail but then leave the meeting without any intention to actually follow the diet regimen. We return the next week to start all over again with more plans, and, in the meantime, we continue to gain weight. Jeremiah said it plainly in the verses I've cited and so will I again:

**STOP! Think about it!** If you are a Baby Boomer then you are at one of the biggest and perhaps final crossroads of your life. You are about to enter into your retirement phase of life. Do you realize that nowhere in the entire Bible is there a reference to retirement or even the concept of retirement? Retirement is not a Biblical concept!

**Stand at the Crossroads! Look at what is before you!** You are about to choose the final major pathway for your life. Will you serve your Creator or yourself? Have you accomplished all that you were designed to accomplish? That's right; God made you according to a set of blueprints, if you will, and on those prints are listed all the potential things you could accomplish. You may not realize that you were given certain "standard equipment" — your talents and gifts — that you have not yet used or developed.

How far have you come? How much is left to do? Pray for an answer. It's not too late to ask and it's not too late to go back and complete what He has meant for you to do. It is never too late to start anew no matter how many times you've tried before.

**Ask instead where the good path is. Find it!** You will probably have to search for this for some time. It is not easily found in today's culture. You could do this with friends, or your spouse, and seek the right path together.

And when you find it, **Walk in it!**

You will find rest for your soul; I guarantee it, and so does God.

*"A smile is the light in your window that tells others that there is a caring, sharing person inside. "*

~ Dennis Waitley (1933-);
writer

# 10

## What's the Real Reason for Going Back?

*"Dare to reach out your hand into the darkness, to pull another hand into the light."*

~Norman B. Rice (1943-);
former mayor of Seattle, Washington

In chapter 7 of this book, I told a story about teaching CCD (Sunday school for Catholic students) to a group of eighth graders, when one of the boys stood up and loudly demanded an explanation as to why he should have to be in the class. After the outburst, he dropped back into his chair with his arms folded and head down. As I said earlier, I had been confronted by an angry 13-year-old and all I could do was stand there with my mouth open. The truth of his words paralyzed me. I just could not think of anything to say that would effectively counter his observations. I thought about this in the days that followed, and the next Sunday I decided to try and answer him in an unusual way.

Once all of the students had arrived, I told them that we would be going over to the church for that day's session. I told them that I prayed all week and that I had asked Jesus to visit us today. Each one was to sit in a pew and I would give them paper and a pencil. I would place a chair at the foot of the altar and after I lit a candle, Jesus would come and sit there. They could talk with Him by writing down whatever they wanted. They were not to put their names on the paper. After I explained this, half the class started to laugh and complain that this was silly and childish, but the other half was silent and I could see that they were thinking.

We got to the church and I placed the chair at the foot of the altar while each student went to a pew. The boy who had been complaining the previous week sat in the very last pew with his arms folded, clearly wanting none of this. I lit the candle and after a short while everyone started writing. I had my back to the altar and was watching the class when the boy in the last pew suddenly jumped up, pointed to the chair, and shouted, "Look!" Bright sunlight had come through one of the stained-glass windows, creating a laser-like shaft of blue light that hit directly dead-center on that chair.

The kids rushed forward and stood staring at that chair, but no one said a word and no one dared to touch the blue light. One by one they quietly went back to their seats and continued to write, but now with more intensity. The boy in the last pew came up to me and sheepishly asked for paper and pencil. He then sat down in the first pew, and began to write. I nearly ran out of paper and pencils that day; the children had a lot to say to Jesus.

I wish I could share those stories with you. A great deal of what they handed in was very painful to read and it just broke my heart to see what was in those letters. Even at 13 years of age, these kids had to deal with many of the same things adults struggle with every day. But they all wanted to believe what I was telling them about God. They wanted to believe it was true, but since there was little or no physical evidence of it in their worlds, they were likely to cast it aside as nonsense. It became clear to me that they do look to their elders to see what is true. What we believe in is what they will believe in and what they will demonstrate in their actions.

When society realizes that a certain species in nature is endangered, it moves to do what it can to protect that species and its habitat. We are put on notice that we need to do all that we can to help repair that habitat and help heal any of the affected members so that they can again be healthy, grow and prosper. We take great measures to help restore that species to its proper position in nature. But if we are honest with ourselves and look objectively at the condition of our youth today, we will see that a great many of them are similarly threatened. They too should be put on the endangered species list.

I mentioned the experience I had at an AA meeting several times throughout this book. I had a discussion with a director of another AA facility that was very revealing. He said that in the "old days" when alcohol was the major substance to which people became addicted, it would take an average of fifteen to twenty plus years before the addiction became apparent to others and required treatment. Now, with the surge in drug use and alcohol in our society, the average incubation period is approximately 18-24 months. The director said that his facility can take in people as young as 18 years of age, but if they were to drop that minimum age to 16, he could at least double the number of residents in the program.

We have all heard these kinds of troubling statistics repeated many times. It has gotten to the point that we have come to accept these conditions as part of normal living today. We reason that it's just the way things are and that we are doing all that we can about it.

In fact, many of us feel that we don't have to do much of anything about these disturbing trends, as long as *there is no God.* After all, we may reason, why bother, as we have discussed, if, in the end, we just die and there is no further consciousness or life after this one? Or perhaps we think there is a God, and He is going to let everyone into Heaven anyway. Why get all stressed out if this is how it all ends?

Some of us older folks may feel badly about all of the problems youths are experiencing, but we justify our inaction by convincing ourselves that we've had our hard times as well, that's just how life works, and these young folks had better get used to it. Is this the correct way to see things? Shouldn't we be reacting differently to the critical condition of our children? Let's think about this a bit further.

At the heart of the Christian message is the story of how God made this world and how Satan then entered that creation and made it his domain. God allowed this to happen because of man's sinful choices. (See 2 Corinthians 4:3-4, Ephesians 2:2, Revelation 12:9.) We first learn this in the story of Adam and Eve. Many scoff at that story, but whether you believe it or not, the spiritual truth that it conveys is real.

Evil is a very real force in the world. We cannot avoid the evidence that our eyes and ears provide to us today as we listen to news reports, and see the issues that our children are struggling with in their lives. After all, if we can believe in a supernatural being called God, why can we not believe in the existence of an opposite creature called Satan? Good and evil both abound in the world around us. Satan's job is to populate Hell, plain and simple. God's job is to get all of His children back home again with Him. That is why He sent His only son, Jesus Christ, to earth.

*For the Son of Man came to seek and to save what was lost.* (Luke 19:10)

The story of Christianity is simple at its core. The world has become corrupted by sin and the activities of Satan and his forces. God is doing all that He can to save us, given that He is hampered by our free will. It is a rescue mission not unlike the situations that we encounter during and after a natural disaster. People can choose to accept their own rescue or not.

It is the same thing with God. We can choose to believe in Him and His laws or not. We have the choice because we have free will. God gave us that when He made us and many people use that gift every day. Therefore, all He can do is *offer* to save us. We have to want that salvation as well. He will not save people against their will. He will never force anyone to go to Heaven after they die. If they lived their lives in a way that clearly showed they had no interest in God or His laws, then it is by their choice that they do not enter Heaven.

My personal goal is to get out of this life alive... and to help as many as I can to do the same. I believe that my mission as a Christian is the same mission that Jesus had, to help save that which was lost. Notice the wording on the above verse. To save what *was* lost. Sin takes us off track from the truth, and we become lost. Many of our children, not to mention those our own age as well, are lost. We have to help save them. Real and true life is believing in Christ because it is through faith that we are carried safely into the life beyond this one.

So there you have it. The real reason for going back, for making that U-turn is not necessarily for your own personal gain or well-being, but rather to help save those that may not make it back on their own. If you decide to go back by making a U-turn, then go back to show your children and others close to you the correct way home. If God thought it was so important that He sent us a personal savior, and since Jesus accepted that mission, then that's reason enough for us to act. We have work to do, and believe it or not, God needs our help. What could be more urgent or clear? What could be more important?

> *If anyone would come after me, he must deny himself and take up his cross and follow me. For whoever wants to save his life will lose it, but whoever loses his life for me and for the gospel will save it.*　　(Mark 8:34-36)

*"Do more than belong: participate. Do more than care: help. Do more than believe: practice. Do more than be fair: be kind. Do more than forgive: forget. Do more than dream: work."*
~ William Arthur Ward (1921-1994);
writer

# 11
## How to Make a Successful U-Turn

*"Encouragement is the oxygen of the soul."*
~ George M. Adams (1837-1920);
US Representative from Kentucky

Melissa was 32 years old and married to Tom, 31, and their beautiful son Thomas was almost two years old. About six or seven months earlier Tom started to feel sick. No medication or therapy he took seemed to help him. He would have good days and then awful days. Test after test came back negative, with everything from Lyme's disease to acid reflux being ruled out. Still, his condition continued to worsen.

Then one particular day, the lymph nodes under his arms and in his neck became swollen. The team of infectious disease doctors he was seeing decided to operate and remove the gland in his neck so they could study it more closely and see what was going on. Their fear was that it might be lymphoma. I went to see Melissa at her office a few days before the operation in order to pray with her. As we talked, a co-worker came into the room and said she woke up that day sensing that she and her husband were to visit Tom and Melissa that evening and pray over him before the surgery took place.

I thought that was a great plan, so I took out two stone pocket crosses and prepared to give them to Melissa. As I was handing them to her, the co-worker's son Peter, who happened to be visiting that day, came into the room with his best friend. They were both nine years old and schoolmates. They saw the crosses and excitedly asked about them. I took out two more and gave them to the boys and explained that these matchbook-sized crosses, carved from various types of stone, are a kind of tool to help us feel that God is always with us. They were thrilled to receive them. That night Peter accompanied his parents when they went to pray over Tom and Melissa. It was a very emotional time for everyone.

The following evening before dinner, Melissa and Tom sat down at the table with two-year-old Thomas between them. They were not in the habit of saying grace before meals but under the circumstances they thought it appropriate to start doing so. The three of them held hands and gave thanks. The next evening as they sat down to dinner and were ready to begin eating, little Thomas looked up at them and held out his hands to his parents. He expected to repeat what they did the night before. Their two-year-old reminded them of what was important, praying together. His behavior that evening was stunning to both of them.

The next day Peter saw his friend Ben at school and suggested they go outside behind the bleachers and pray for Tom. So these two nine-year-old boys, with their stone pocket crosses, went before God (on public school property no less) and asked Him to heal Tom. Several days later the tests came back, and, while they were partially inconclusive, the doctors were still able to rule out the threat of cancer. When Peter was told that Tom did not have cancer, his response to his mother was simply "Yeah, I already knew that, Mom. After that man gave us the crosses, Ben and I prayed together behind the bleachers the other day and God said that He would heal Tom and we believed Him."

*....unless you change and become like little children...*

(Matthew 18:3)

The story does not end there, however. A week or so after the good news from his surgery, Tom decided to return his pocket cross to me. He was suddenly and miraculously back to his old self, so he thought I could pass it along to someone else who needed it more than him. But I simply refused to take it back. He was shocked, but I insisted that *he* should pass it along to someone else who might need it. He accepted the challenge but I could see that he was reluctant to do so. Well, it was just two weeks later when he was informed that one of his closest co-workers had been diagnosed with stage-two cancer.

Tom and many others at the school where he taught were devastated by the news. He struggled over whether he should give the pocket cross to this woman. He was afraid that since they were both public school teachers that perhaps the cross would be inappropriate, or, more likely, that his friend would not accept it. He feared that giving her the cross would not be the politically correct thing to do. So he continued to agonize over it for another week.

Finally, he decided to give her a card, and in it he wrote what the cross meant to him and how it had helped him. He gave her the card and the cross. Her reaction was powerfully emotional, as you might imagine. She was overwhelmed by his words and his gift. Through her tears she told Tom that she was waiting for a sign from God and that little cross was it. Tom's faith took a quantum leap that day.

Consider this: after a battery of tests, your doctor confirms that you have a serious disease which will probably shorten your life considerably and may begin to affect you at any time. What is it that you would want most at that point? Is it money, a vacation, a new car? No, I think you would want to be healed. Doctors and medicines certainly can help us, but once we get to a point in our lives where we are facing a life-threatening disease, how we perceive things can change very quickly.

The realization that this life may suddenly end can open up a portal into the future where we can see what might be ahead for us. The next life comes into view along with all of the questions surrounding it. It can be very frightening, and that is when many of us start to look for the only One who can help. When this has happened to people I've known, I have found that those simple little pocket crosses can help a great deal.

Tom took a big step when he gave that cross to his friend. For him it was unlike anything he had ever done. His actions reminded me of the story of the Good Samaritan (see Luke 10:30). Tom decided to stop and go back to that person that needed help, and he gave her what she probably needed most at that moment in her life. Tom made a U-turn, and I was very proud of him. Many lives were, and will probably continue to be, touched by his action. He did what Jesus did.

Our model for how we make these U-turns, therefore, is Jesus Himself. We must remember that when He walked the earth, as he neared each town He could have very easily just stood atop a hill and waved His hands in a grand sweeping motion declaring that everyone in the town be healed, well fed and cared for. But He didn't do that. He *personally* visited everyone that He could, and listened. He answered their questions and their needs. He demonstrated to us what true Christianity is: a one-on-one encounter with needy people in our lives and our positive response to their needs.

Unfortunately for us, there is no cookie-cutter template that describes how best to make a U-turn. One size does not fit all. As in the case of Tom, none of us involved could have anticipated all of the things that were to occur. But I've learned that the first step in making a good U-turn is to yield to God's will as represented by His Holy Spirit. Jesus did this in His life's work. He yielded to the will of His Father. Let God direct your steps in the U-turn process. All you have to do is to present yourself as willing and ready to do as He says. But you must be very connected to Him. You must be able to recognize His voice in the form of His Holy Spirit.

This has been the most difficult chapter in the book for me to write. It's difficult because whenever someone proposes a great idea or notion, people want to know how it can be applied to real life. Naturally we want to see the step-by-step directions that are required in order to be successful with this new proposal. We all want and need the details, action plans, steps to take and all the answers to who, what, where, when and how. But unfortunately that is not how making a U-turn works. Remember when Jesus sent out His disciples to different towns and cities to represent Him, they went with very little by way of money, resources, or instructions. They did go two by two, but they had to figure out things as they encountered them. More accurately, they had to rely on God's Holy Spirit for guidance, and so it is with us. This perhaps is the hardest part about the process of making a U-turn. God will be our new GPS system and we will have to trust Him.

I have learned (oftentimes the hard way) that when God wants me to do something, He does not give me the whole picture. He gives it to me in pieces. He breaks it down into small chunks or steps and feeds these pieces to me slowly and He's usually very quiet. So I have to listen carefully all the time. And

I'm not good at that. I'm the kind of person that needs first to see the big picture, and then I want all the specifics on how something needs to be done. I want to get all of this information immediately, and then I am impatient for the results. However, I have learned (and am still learning) to be patient and "wait on the Lord." He's driving the bus, if you will, and we're along for the ride.

Let me tell you where the pocket cross idea came from and why I use them. I came to realize over time that I needed some kind of a physical tool that could help me when I came across people who needed to connect with God. When I would counsel people in my practice regarding tax matters and finances, they would tell me things of a personal nature that would oftentimes defy a financial solution. Serious medical issues, marriage problems, addictions, and child and parent difficulties would eventually reveal themselves in these conversations. Since these issues almost always had a financial impact on their families and businesses, I would hear about them sooner or later. Sometimes it would get to the point where I'd be reluctant to ask people how they were doing for fear that they would tell me the truth!

I came across these stone pocket crosses about eight years ago on the Internet. They are made by some wonderful people in California. I found that when discussing the overwhelming challenges that people were facing, it seemed that the only way to deal effectively with it was to present them with something that reminded them that spiritual help is always available. So I would simply offer them a stone cross. After handing out nearly one thousand crosses, no one so far has refused to accept one. As a lady who was raised in the Jewish faith recently said to me, as she accepted the cross, "You know, I never told a soul about this, but this is so interesting: I always felt that Jesus was my friend."

Having something tangible to hang onto as we move through the challenges of the day is important. And knowing that these crosses are connected to the only One that can help us can be very comforting. We are like children in that regard. My two-year-old grandson loves his stuffed elephant; it goes with him wherever he goes. Remember Linus with his blanket in the cartoon strip *Peanuts?* In a similar vein, the stone pocket crosses have given many people a deep sense of personal security in Jesus Christ, especially during their times of crisis.

However, the crosses are merely a tool. There is nothing magical about them. The power lies in what and Whom they represent. So I give them out at the right moment and I try to rely on the urging of the Holy Spirit to guide me as to when I should give one to someone. There have been a number of times when I did not offer a cross even though the conversation I was having had a serious tone. The crosses have been most effective when given at a moment of crisis in a person's life. There are other tools a person can use to help people see the truth in a situation and to help them make a U-turn. For me though, the crosses have worked very well.

To me, Tom's story is simply beautiful. He was in serious need, and look at how others came together around and alongside him to support him. Even his two-year-old son was motivated to join in at a critical moment. How does that happen? It happens when God sees us trying to restore people and things in their lives. His Holy Spirit enters the situation and then orchestrates and provides the help we all need. In fact, all we have to do sometimes is just show up. Make the effort to support someone in need and you will find more often than not that God will do the heavy lifting. The faith of everyone in Tom's story was changed and deepened. I was honored to be a part of it.

*The best way to find yourself is to lose yourself in the service of others.* ~ Mohandas Karamchand Gandhi (1869-1948)

You may be wondering about me. Have I made a U-turn yet? I believe I have — more than a few times. Let me explain what happened in one particular area of my life. It was around 1980 when both of our children were born. At this very time I decided to go off on my own and start a CPA firm. It was a big step for me, and the riskiest thing I had ever tried. My focus was entirely on making that firm a success. Unfortunately, it monopolized all of my attention and I was rarely at home to help my wife with our very young children.

I had played a lot of golf when I was young, so now a business associate suggested that I join a local golf club in order to gain more clients and get some exercise. This sounded logical to me so I signed up. From that point on, if I was not at the office, at a client's place of business, or at some other business related function, I was on the golf course. It left precious little time to be at home to help out.

As I look back now, spending that time away from my family is probably the greatest regret of my life. It was not until some twenty years later that I realized what I had done. Using the excuse that I needed to develop the accounting practice, I made sure that I was not at home to help my wife and children as they encountered the challenges of their daily lives.

After this revelation finally dawned on me, it added to my desire to find a tool to help me have a more permanent and meaningful impact in peoples' lives. That's when I found the pocket crosses and they have helped me accomplish this. It was my way of making up for the lost opportunities with my family and others in the past. But, as I said earlier, it was hard to go back at that point. The children had grown up and were headed in different directions. Yet I still tried to make myself available to my family. I also started to look to the future for those I could help currently. I wanted to "pay it forward," if you will. Yes, I did make a U-turn back then, and I resolved to do what I could to help those around me. I can tell you now that it was one of the best things I have ever done.

Interestingly, an opportunity at a local university presented itself at the same time and I began to teach accounting and financial literacy courses to young folks. This, too, has turned out to be a U-turn-type moment in my life. What I did not give my own children when they were young, I now could give to the young folks that came to my classes. As for the relationship with my wife, we found a way to spend the weekends together, something I never pursued in the past. We found some common interests and rediscovered that God knew what He was doing when He brought us together some 40 years earlier. God is good.

U-turns are really second, third, fourth, and so on, chances. They present themselves often enough in life. We just have to make up our minds whether or not we want to take advantage of them when they occur. It's not always easy to do. But knowing that you are doing the right thing is very redeeming and a great feeling. Redemption and forgiveness are wonderful things that we are continually in need of and they come straight from God. Oftentimes He uses His Holy Spirit to encourage us to deliver these gifts to others. That too is an incredible feeling to experience. When you can help others feel forgiven, and even redeemed, after something they did that may have hurt others, it is what I call being in the "God Zone." It's a little like playing a sport where you just seem incapable of making an error or a bad shot. Being "in the zone" is a rare event and very exhilarating.

In addition to the Holy Spirit, the 21st-century Christian will need to rely on, among other things, real life stories to help others find their way home. The stories I have compiled from these pocket crosses are very real and they are effective tools in helping people see the truth. As I mentioned earlier, the truth today is hard to discern mainly because we as a nation have been pre-occupied for so long with what amounts to "make believe" beliefs. Instead of seeking out real truth every day as it relates to our lives, we have lost sight of it. We let it get away from us.

Our children need to clearly understand that difference between right and wrong as they try to make the right choices in their lives. Because of our short short-sightedness and the fact that, in acting this way, we've been on the wrong road for so long, we have served them poorly, and in short we may have done them great harm.

When a particular behavior or experience continues to yield good outcomes or at least consistent results, we tend to start thinking of it as a "truth." We can then take those truths and clearly identify the best practices in our lives which lead us to make better choices. That is one reason why I have focused on Baby Boomers in this book. By now we as a generation have gone through the bulk of our lives. We should know what works well and what does not.

For example, we should be telling young folks about the practical realities of drug use. We should be telling them what to look for when contemplating marriage. We should be telling them how devastating a divorce can be to a family, especially to its younger members. But we need to tell them these things from *our own personal experiences.* They must hear and see where *we* personally went wrong and they must hear it directly from us.

There are many books written on these matters. But they are not enough. Today we have very few older folks willing to stand up, admit publically where they made big mistakes in life, and share their personal stories with the hope that they will help others. Alcoholics Anonymous uses this technique and it works. Remember "show and tell?" We learned that concept in the first grade. It is time to reinstate it for all adults! That's how we can make a good U-turn. We can start investing ourselves in other peoples' lives.

Jesus Christ made a personal investment in mankind. If you add up all of the personal sacrifices made by people since the beginning of time, they would not even register in comparison to what He did for us. It is not the quantity of your investment that counts but instead that you chose to take a vested interest in another human being, as He did. If we decide to make a U-turn and go back to fix, repair, restore or improve a relationship with someone, then we will have to be willing to give it all we have, just like Jesus did. I have come to believe that this is the most important thing we need to do now, for ourselves, for our generation and for all of the people born after us. It is extremely important, and no matter what it costs us personally, as they say in the military, "it is a good hill to die on."

Let me make this point again, but this time from God's perspective. Jesus gave us two great commandments: to love God with all of our mind, heart, strength and soul; and to love our neighbor as ourselves (see Luke 10:27). Lots of people know these verses of Scripture and consequently have come to call them "the two great commandments." In addition, there is a somewhat lesser known, but related, passage in 1 John 4:20:

*If anyone says, "I love God," yet hates his brother, he is a liar. For anyone who does not love his brother, whom he*

173

*has seen, cannot love God, whom he has not seen. And*
*He has given us this command: Whoever loves God must*
*also love his brother.*                    (1 John 4:20)

I have discovered that there is a third commandment hidden within the above statements. I can express it this way: we are to (1) love God, (2) love one another *(3) as we love ourselves.* Thus, we are to love God, but in order to love God we must love our brothers and sisters. We are instructed to love one another *as we love ourselves.* If we do not love ourselves correctly, how can we love others correctly, and therefore, how can we love God correctly?

Can you see the problem? Many of us go about doing "work for the Lord" while harboring ill will toward others, or even toward ourselves. How many times have you heard someone say "Oh, I'll never forgive myself for that?" Well, you must forgive yourself if you want to be of use to God! In addition, if we do not take care of ourselves with regard to how we eat, drink, think, believe, act and so on, then how can we truly love anyone else *as* we love ourselves? We can't do this, if we don't love ourselves in the correct way!

When Jesus was walking the earth some 2000 years ago, it was said that He spent most of His ministry years healing, repairing, restoring, teaching, and, in general, *loving* those He came across every day. His followers must have regarded Him as the "superman" of their day. Yet incredibly, He was plucked from their midst, tortured and hung on a wooden cross to die. What must have gone through the minds of His followers in the days that followed His death? Whatever they thought, they had two paths from which to choose as to what they should do.

First, they could have simply said "enough!" They were not sure what happened or why but their personal responsibilities and livelihoods and families had to be attended to. With that, they could have left and gone home, back to their businesses, work and families.

Secondly, they could stop, "pull over to the side of the road," if you will, and think about making a U-turn. Interestingly, they were on the right road following Jesus while He was alive and in their presence. But now that He was gone, the road would have to change; the mission would have to be altered to meet new demands and circumstances. This is exactly what they did; they realized how important Christ's messages were and they began to write His words and actions down. This is where the New Testament comes from.

His disciples decided to go back and review the lessons He had taught them and the events they had witnessed. During this time God revealed his Holy Spirit and peoples' lives were changed forever. The first century church was born. This new Christian church exploded in love and care for each of its members as well as for all mankind.

Small groups developed in far-off places, all focused on helping one another. Sometimes meetings were held in secret locations due to the persecution the followers experienced. They took God's words to heart and gave them life through their actions. They made a giant U-turn and look what happened: history itself was changed.

These early Christians, then, are the model for those of us who would choose to be known as 21st-century Christians. In order to go forward as followers of Christ, we need to first go back, make that U-turn, and rediscover the basics of our faith. We are to study how the Christian faith was propagated in the first, second and third centuries after Christ. Then we are to import those techniques and beliefs into the 21st century while allowing for modern day changes in society and technology. I believe this will work because basic human nature has not changed all that much over the course of history, and today we are as desperate as Christ's earliest followers were after they lost Him.

We hear a similar argument today regarding our current political system. There are those who now calling for a return to the principles and core values of our Founding Fathers in America. They say that if we want to move forward successfully, we do not have to "reinvent the wheel." Our ancestors invented the best practices many years ago, whether we are talking about running our government, our lives, or matters of faith. As 21st-century Christians, we just have to make up our minds whether we want to use those best practices or not. Do we want to re-invent the wheel in terms of how best to live with one another? It is not necessary. That wheel was invented long ago.

To be successful we must also have a full understanding of our motivation in making that U-turn. Are we doing it for personal gain? Are we doing it out of guilt and not love? Are we being forced to do it by someone else? These are some of the wrong reasons to make a U-turn, and if we allow such reasons to motivate us, we will fail even as we begin.

In my own case, when I finally woke up to the reality of how my behavior affected those closest to me, I welcomed the opportunity to make that U-turn. I did have a sense of guilt in me but it was not the main motivating force for my U-turn. I realized I had cheated the people I loved most and it was my love for them that helped me go back to do what I could to make things right.

Once again, I think this is the best reason we can have for making the U-turn. Jesus' mission was "to save that which was lost." Notice His phrasing. He came to save that which was (*already*) lost. Sin kidnaps us and gets us lost. It takes us far from our Father. The wage of sin is death (see Romans 6:23). For us today, that means we are in trouble, and not just a little bit. This especially applies to many of us older folks.

If we can finally admit to ourselves that we are in trouble, do we want to do anything about it? There are probably lots of reasons, or excuses, why we cannot or will not take action. But are our reasons and excuses valid in God's eyes? If we are too preoccupied with running our own lives, and looking first for material gain in everything we do, then remember something else He said to us:

> *What good will it be for a man if he gains the whole world, yet forfeits his soul? Or what can a man give in exchange for his soul? For the Son of Man is going to come in his Father's glory with his angels, and then he will reward each person according to what he has done.*
>
> (Matt 16:26-27)

I just love this question: suppose Jesus were to suddenly show up on your doorstep and announce that He would like to shadow your daily actions for the next month or so. He'll go to work with you, He'll recreate with you, He'll listen to your phone conversations and He'll know your thoughts, and every detail of your daily life. How much of what you routinely do every day would suddenly change? Do you think He would approve of your everyday activities and behavior?

He wants us to prosper, there's no doubt about that. But if the mission of Christ was to save souls, then wouldn't He be seeking some evidence of our worthiness in our daily actions?

What would Jesus witness us doing on an average day that contributes to someone else's personal salvation, improvement or restoration?

In return, what would you get from this experience with Him? I would hope that you would feel His passion for His mission to save and restore those around us. I would hope that you would see the rescue mission that He is on and I would hope that you would now want to join in with Him more actively. These are not small questions and thoughts; they are the big ones that we need to answer for ourselves, and *time is running out for many of us.*

So here it is: the way home, the way to successfully proceed into the future, is to go back and relearn what Jesus' followers discovered some 2000 years ago. The path we need to take is the same one that they took back then. The first step is to make a U-turn for ourselves. We must begin by properly loving ourselves again. For too many years, many of us Boomers have been abusing ourselves.

The second step is all about educating those around us about Jesus Christ. Then it's about helping to repair, fix, heal, and restore the lives of those we encounter every day. Give people the benefit of your life experience. Tell them what you've discovered to be the best practices in whatever area of life you are discussing. Give them a gift of your love, and, yes, it helps if it includes something tangible like a stone pocket cross that they can hang onto in their times of crisis.

The process may be simply handing them that pocket cross or taking them to have coffee and listening to their concerns. It may be that their troubles are beyond your ability to help, but, like the Good Samaritan, you can lift them up and bring them to a place where others can help them find healing. We can pray with and over people and ask the Holy Spirit to heal them. After all, what power is greater than the Holy Spirit?

We need to really start caring about people. Sometimes that means writing a check, but more often it means to stop what we are doing and help a person you know, or perhaps one you don't know that well. If they are hurting and they need help, that's all that matters. Their suffering qualifies them for our personal concern and our help.

The "Followers of the Way" some 2000 years ago discovered this for themselves. This is where many ministries and churches stop in their efforts to do Christ's work; we are very quick to respond with money and materials when people are in need, but to respond with an unlimited amount of our time and personal attention is quite another thing.

For the majority of people, including myself, this kind of commitment often seems too much. Many of us will respond to this part of our Christian walk as the rich young ruler did in the Scriptures. He turned and walked away from Jesus when faced with the decision to sell all that he had, give it to the poor and follow Christ (see Luke 18:18-25). Changing this is the final and most critical step in our U-turn process, and the step that is holding Christianity back from growing exponentially as it did in the early church years.

But now that must change... *we* must change. Listen to how *The Purpose Driven Life* author Pastor Rick Warren puts it:

### The Angel Stadium Declaration, April 2005
Today I am stepping across the line. I'm tired of waffling, and I'm finished with wavering. I've made my choice; the verdict is in; and my decision is irrevocable. I'm going God's way. There's no turning back now!

I will live the rest of my life serving God's purposes with God's people on God's planet for God's glory. I will use my life to celebrate his presence, cultivate his character, participate in his family, demonstrate his love, and communicate his Word.

Since my past has been forgiven, and I have a purpose for living and a home awaiting in heaven, I refuse to waste any more time or energy on shallow living, petty thinking, trivial talking, thoughtless doing, useless regretting, hurtful resenting, or faithless worrying. Instead I will magnify God, grow to maturity, serve in ministry, and fulfill my mission in the membership of his family.

Because this life is preparation for the next, I will value worship over wealth, "we" over "me," character over comfort, service over status, and people over possessions, position, and pleasures. I know what matters most and I'll give it all I've got. I'll do the best I can with what I have for Jesus Christ today.

I won't be captivated by culture, manipulated by critics, motivated by praise, frustrated by problems, debilitated by temptation, or intimidated by the devil. I'll keep running my race with my eyes on the goal, not the sidelines or those running by me. When times get tough and I get tired, I won't back up, back off, back down, back out, or backslide. I'll just keep moving forward by God's grace. I'm Spirit-led, purpose-driven, and mission-focused, so I cannot be bought, I will not be compromised, and I shall not quit until I finish the race.

I'm a trophy of God's amazing grace so I will be gracious to everyone, grateful for every day, and generous with everything that God entrusts to me.

To my Lord and Savior Jesus Christ, I say: However,

whenever, wherever, and whatever you ask me to do, my answer in advance is yes! Wherever you lead and whatever the cost, I'm ready. Anytime. Anywhere. Any way. Whatever it takes Lord; whatever it takes! I want to be used by you in such a way that on that final day I'll hear you say, "Well done, thou good and faithful one. Come on in, and let the eternal party begin!"

Do you hear the sense of urgency in his words? Do you hear his weary response to doing things the same old way? Do you hear him saying that he's had enough of the road he is on and so should we? It has been the wrong road all along. If it was the correct road, we would now be in much better condition as a society. It is time for a U-turn.

There is even more evidence that this conclusion is correct. Consider again the following verse of Scripture from Luke in which Jesus talks about saving just one lost sheep.

> *Then Jesus told them this parable: : "Suppose one of you has a hundred sheep and loses one of them. Does he not leave the ninety-nine in the open country and go after the lost sheep until he finds it? And when he finds it, he joyfully puts it on his shoulders and goes home. Then he calls his friends and neighbors together and says, 'Rejoice with me; I have found my lost sheep.' I tell you that in the same way there will be more rejoicing in heaven over one sinner who repents than over ninety-nine righteous persons who do not need to repent."* (Luke 15:3-7)

Every time I come across these words I am reminded as to how far we have "progressed" in our culture. In today's world it seems that the numbers are switched. It is more likely that we have one sheep safely located in the pasture and ninety-nine lost out in the hills somewhere.

Many people who have lived in our country through the last 50 or more years of the 20th century have experienced a goodly amount of prosperity. They have used their wealth to indulge themselves in all kinds of pleasures, some to the point of addiction. Now they are lost and need to be found. Who will undertake this work? For those of us who know the Lord, who claim to be Jesus' followers, the call is as clear and urgent as it could possibly be. And time is running out, for all of us.

It was Henry David Thoreau who said, *"Men live lives of quiet desperation."* That was very true when he first said it and it is even truer today. Many of us experience this feeling of desperation because of the bad choices we have made. As Jesus' followers, our call then is to come alongside those that we encounter every day and invest ourselves in the people we know. That is exactly what Jesus did, and for that matter so did the members of the early church in the years after Christ's death.

In one sense, what we have to do now is not "rocket science." But in another sense it is probably the hardest thing we will ever attempt. Why? Because most of us are not set up to do this kind of work. Sometimes it is a lot easier to help a stranger than it is to help a relative or someone you've known for a long time.

For the majority of our lives, we have invested almost all of our time and resources into our careers, our immediate family and closest friends and our own entertainment. The fact is that helping people we know well or not at all, or personally walking someone back from the "edge" where they were about to make a tragic mistake is something many of us are untrained and unready to do. Furthermore, our politically correct culture tells us to mind our own business.

But there's hope. We can choose to make a U-turn. We can decide to learn and change in the process. We can use our free will as an asset that will help us do the right thing. That is what this book is all about, helping you see what you can do even if it is not part of the popular thinking and culture.

If you wish to move forward successfully in the years you have left, remember this:

*People don't care how much you know until they know how much you care.*

**Let's review.** If we want to go back, if we want to make that U-turn, we need to first start with ourselves. It's not that we're supposed to be in love with ourselves, but rather it's how we care for our own bodies, minds, hearts and souls. We should care because these are God's gifts to us. And remember, these gifts are not standardized in the sense that everyone has the same gifts and talents. Each of us is endowed with special talents and abilities that are designed so we can interact with others. In a way we are all like pieces to the same puzzle. Together we make up the big picture. Without all of the pieces, the puzzle is not complete.

We need to care about ourselves because we're going to need all of our resources so that we are in good shape to be successful in life and to do God's will and work. We then have to look around us, both in the present and into the past, and see whom we need to help today and who we should have helped yesterday, last year or even further back in the past.

For some of us it may be different. Perhaps we are at a point in our lives where we still have not yet fulfilled our greatest potential or purpose. The U-turn could help us remember a dream or desire that we once had, which, over time, became improbable and faded away. Maybe God called us to a task in the past and we have not answered. Maybe we can answer him now; it is not too late.

As I mentioned earlier, a great question to help guide us on this journey is "What would Jesus do?" But I have found that a better question is "What *did* Jesus do?" It's better because it eliminates the speculation and forces us to do the research. We are then driven to His Word in the Bible, especially the Gospels, where we will find what He actually did, and why.

There are commentaries and explanations written by knowledgeable people that can help us understand. When we seek the Lord, He will answer us and when that happens, the Holy Spirit can then better influence and guide our lives.

As for techniques and methods to apply in making your U-turn, you can follow the Gospels. Take a look at the kind of things Jesus did and the kind of stories He told. Look at the story of the Good Samaritan (Luke 10:30) for example. Re-read the story of the paralytic (Mark 2:1) who wanted to see Jesus but could not get close enough because of the crowds, and his four friends made a hole in the thatched roof of the house where Jesus was and lowered him down into His presence. These are great examples of being invested in the people around you. Remember, the focus should always be on restoration and repair.

Another technique is to find someone else who would like to take this journey with you. Even Jesus needed twelve disciples to help Him. And pray....*pray like you've never prayed before.* You can go nowhere without His help (John 15:5). These are critical lessons to learn.

Ever since I discovered the pocket crosses I keep a few in

my pocket at all times. They are big and coarse enough to remind me that they are there. This way, whenever I meet someone, in the back of my mind I am trying to find out if they are someone who needs a cross. It keeps me connected to God on a personal level and it helps me pay real attention to the person in front of me.

And finally, as you read the four Gospels, I would recommend that you pay attention to the sense you get about the heart of Christ. What was He doing when He healed and fed and repaired people? Why would He do that? After all, His principle mission was to die for us and redeem mankind. He could have accomplished that in one week. But He also made sure He spent a great deal of time walking about and doing all manner of good things. Once again, that's what He wanted us to learn and copy. He was modeling for us, and we need to do the same for the younger folks today.

And before you say that this is all beyond your ability to do, remember what He told us before He left to return to Heaven...

*I tell you the truth, anyone who has faith in me will do what I have been doing. He will do even greater things than these, because I am going to the Father. And I will do whatever you ask in my name, so that the Son may bring glory to the Father. You may ask me for anything in my name, and I will do it.* (John 14:12-14)

Let me end this chapter with one more personal story involving the stone pocket crosses. This was a defining moment in my life and I shall never forget it.

A number of years ago, I attended a three-day Christian conference in Connecticut. The organizers brought in a band to provide us with Christian music. There was a particular singer in that group named Carol. She had an incredible voice. I spoke with her during a break and found out that she was going through some very tough times. Still, her faith in God was sustaining her. I gave her a stone pocket cross and we prayed together. She then listened to my story and politely smiled as I finished. I had the uneasy feeling that there was something else she wanted to tell me but was hesitant since she really didn't know me.

The next day, as I was having lunch with some friends at a busy local diner, Carol came in with her band members and sat at the table next to ours. She smiled at me and took out her cross and held it up for all to see. Everyone talked about it for a while and then things became quiet.

Then from across her table Carol said to me, "Hey Paul, if you will come over here and stand next to me, I'll stand up and sing a song for Jesus."

At first I thought she was joking and I tried to laugh it off, but the look on her face was anything but humorous. Everyone at both of our tables had stopped eating and was looking at me. It suddenly dawned on me that I was being challenged, to stand up publicly for Christ. I wouldn't have to say or do anything but just stand there while she sang *a cappella* in a crowded diner during lunch.

The diner was filled with people of all ages. I was frozen in place, glued to my chair, and just couldn't bring myself to stand up. That's when I felt the nudge, a certain feeling that seemed to say, *"do this for Me."*

Somehow I was able to stand up, and I went over to Carol and stood there next to her. I don't remember what she sang. All I remember was that it was about her love for the Lord. I don't think I ever heard a more sweet and tender song. Everything came to a stop in that diner while she sang. People came out of the kitchen, including the chefs, and customers came from the other side of the diner to listen.

When she was done singing, there was a deafening burst of applause. And that's when she looked at me with tears in her eyes and said, "This is what I wanted to tell you yesterday. But I was hoping I could show you instead, because seeing and hearing is believing. If we don't tell them and show them about Jesus, how will they ever know?"

*"If a man be gracious and courteous to strangers, it shows he is a citizen of the world, and that his heart is no island cut off from other lands, but a continent that joins to them."*

~ Sir Frances Bacon (1561-1626);
philosopher, essayist, statesman

# 12

## The Role of the 21st-Century Christian Church

*"If you talk to a man in a language he understands, that goes to his head. If you talk to him in his language, that goes to his heart."*

~ Nelson Mandela (1918-);
former President of South Africa

If you have reached this point in the book, then you know we have to talk about the current status of our churches. Our churches are supposed to represent a spiritual home base for people of faith. When we consider all of the issues that we have discussed, however, it is reasonable to assume that, in order to accomplish a genuinely successful U-turn, there is much that must change in our Christian churches. So far, we have been focusing solely on individuals who need to make a U-turn and how that may be accomplished. I think we may need to broaden our scope.

For many centuries, churches have been in the forefront of society in upholding the standards of right living. Morality and ethical codes of behavior traditionally have emanated from our mainline churches, both in print and in the pulpit. But in the last 10 to 20 years or so things have changed drastically. We see fewer and fewer people attending services these days, and, most notably, a declining number of young folks.

Many articles and stories have been written about this trend. There are numerous reasons for the declining attendance, but the main point I wish to make is that this is unlikely to be a temporary condition that will correct itself in the near future. Instead, it is probably better characterized as a conscious move away from the Christian God of the Bible.

In a related development, more and more people, both young and old, are getting comfortable with creating their own religious belief systems. I believe this trend is a direct result of the consumerist mindset we've fostered for so long now, and the fact that we in the Boomer generation have done little to change or to stop it.

Consumerism has conditioned us so that we have come to expect that the products and services we need each day are customized and shaped for our own personal use. The result is that we have also extended these expectations to issues of faith and assume that our spiritual needs can be met by "cherry-picking" and by customizing the beliefs we like best.

The situation is very ironic. Not long ago it was we, the individuals, who went through the process of becoming "born again" and after that, we would become members of an established church. Now with this eye toward customization, it is God who is reborn or remade. Our faith, such as it is, is now reconstructed to fit our exact needs and wants, and we can remake the image of God to suit our own wants as well.

In years past we would hear of "cafeteria Catholics" who would pick and choose their beliefs much as you would lunch items in a cafeteria. The term fit because an alarming number of Catholics were choosing to believe the church doctrines they liked and to disregard the ones they did not like. Then a wave of progressivism hit the Protestant denominations, leaving them in a state of confusion with little agreement on what is right and wrong. They too have been in the midst of a "cafeteria" experience. In any event, it seems fewer and fewer members of our churches, leaders and parishioners alike, are certain as to what is right and wrong. The resulting confusion has also hastened the development of the faith customization practices we are witnessing.

I am willing to predict that our churches, in the not-too-distant future, will bear little resemblance, if any, to the ones we attend now. In the 21st century, in order for a church to survive it will have to become, in a word, *relevant*. (I hear this constantly from young folks.) Life has become so frantic and difficult, that if church leaders want people to attend and believe, they have to offer something more than just platitudes and nice words.

Yes, we have the Scriptures, the sacraments, and religious customs, and there is always power in the Word. But many young people don't feel the power. As one young person put it to me, "Well, I don't go to church because I don't see the difference in behavior between the person that goes regularly and the person that does not. And as for it making a person feel better on the inside, I have my music and I have my 'medication' that helps me along."

It is hard to hear this kind of talk but we must allow that today's young folks have grown up in an environment filled with all kinds of accessible pleasures and sensory distractions. Add to that the easy access to drugs and alcohol, and by comparison, what takes place in a church on the weekends will seem boring to them, to say the least. On top of these discouragements, many of our church services are repetitive, ritualistic in their presentation and incomprehensible to those in attendance. We must also remember that we have raised our children to be the ultimate consumers. Younger folks today know how to buy things.

They know where the value is, and so they look for it. It is hard for them to see the value in going to church.

Many believe that all they need to do to be good Christians is to show up at a Mass or church service. As long as they are there, they have fulfilled the requirements of their religion. You become a "good Christian" as long as you show up. Such an approach probably seems silly and unbelievable, particularly to young people, so they perceive church as a waste of time and do not attend.

However, we don't necessarily need to change the format or presentation of our faith and worship services to attract new people. We need to re-examine the reasons *why* we get together at church services. We need to recapture what motivated the early Christians. Even more importantly, we need to rediscover what all true Christians should believe. I think it was St. Francis of Assisi who once said, "Always preach the Gospel and when necessary use words."

The Gospel of the 21st-century church will have to become relevant. It will have to become more meaningful, like the Gospel of the 1st century, involving each one of us on a more fundamental and personal level. Words are good, but our good actions will speak louder and more effectively than our good words.

In chapter six, I mentioned that our generation of Baby Boomers was to blame for taking down all of the "fencing" that marked the established pathways people could follow in developing successful careers, families and lifestyles. Those old pathways and guide lanes are still there, but are hidden under many years of neglect and debris. Like roads that are closed off from general traffic and use, they become unreliable and unusable due to potholes, washouts, and neglect.

Here then is the challenge for today's church hierarchy: we need leaders who can show us the old paths that Jeremiah spoke of and help to open them up again for general public use. We need people who are willing to stand up and show us, by their words and examples, the right pathways to follow.

As we noted in chapter nine, Jesus characterized these paths as follows:

> *Enter through the narrow gate. For wide is the gate and broad is the road that leads to destruction, and many enter through it. But small is the gate and narrow the road that leads to life, and only a few find it.*
>
> (Matthew 7:13-14)

The roads that lead to success are seldom travelled, even in times of revival. But for times such as we are experiencing now, these old paths have become virtually unknown. They need to be redefined and promoted. This is a job for our leaders, with our help. If they cannot or will not do it for some reason, then the task falls directly to those of us who want to develop a new early church of the 21st century.

If our leaders cannot lead, then we need to understand why, and look first to help them. While growing up Catholic, I often wondered who takes care of the "shepherds." How do the clergy stay on the right road and paths? Now we know that many are under great pressure these days to keep their balance in life, and many do it with relatively little help and support from anyone. They are truly the most endangered of all species. This situation will have to be among the first things addressed by members of the new early church of the 21st century. Let's analyze some of the early church history to see how it relates to us today.

In the years immediately following Christ's death on the cross, the newly formed Christian Church began to explode and grow exponentially. How could that happen? The followers' teacher, healer, preacher and leader had just been murdered. By rights, this should have destroyed the movement, relegating it to being a mere footnote in history. But instead it grew, even with severe persecution from the Roman government. Yes, the early followers had the Holy Spirit among them after Pentecost, but so do we today. They had no advantage over Christians today. In many ways we have more physical assets and resources that can, in addition to the Holy Spirit, help us reach people for Christ today.

What was it that made people want to become Christians at a time when doing so was not only unfashionable, but also very dangerous? The followers of Christ simply did what He told them to do before He left: they took care of one another. For example, they met each other's needs as if they were related by marriage or blood. They sacrificed themselves by going into the big, plague-ridden cities. They offered to care for the sick at the risk of catching the disease themselves. Many followers perished as a result.

This is the kind of sacrifice the common person saw when Christianity was at its best. Yes, there was preaching, teaching and praying, but the preaching, teaching and praying came alive as real Christian love in the actions of those early Christians. They truly cared for one another on a personal level. They helped one another not because they were nice people, but out of love for God, and by extension, love for one another. And that has to be at the very core of the new early church of the 21st century; it is truly about our caring for one another, on a one-to-one basis.

Actually the early followers were not known as Christians

until many years later. That title came into being sometime later in the first century. We know that those who came immediately after Christ were called "Followers of the Way." Notice the use of the word "Way." In many of our discussions in this book we have noted that young people these days have a hard time finding their way in life. We have also noted that many of us older folks have been on the wrong road or "way" ourselves.

We need to discover the "Way" once again. And once we find it, we have to walk in the Way. People need to see us living in the Way and see how it benefits us and positively affects those around us. We can talk and preach all we want; we can write all the books we want; and we can hold Bible studies and large Christian conferences every day of the week. But if we do not walk in the Way, then no amount of talking will convince others to join us. And most importantly, the unconvinced are then unlikely to meet Christ. Like it was 2000 years ago, our faith needs to become relevant again. Our faith needs to be reborn.

If, then, we are not along the "Way" where God wants us to be, then where exactly are we? The story of the Prodigal Son represents exactly where we are today. He is the poster child for us in the 21st century. Over the last 40 or 50 years, many of us have gone off to "do our own things" and in the process we have moved very, very far from God. We have lived our lives as we have chosen. We have married and remarried. We have abused alcohol and drugs. We have abused one another at work and at home. Most egregious of all, we have abused our children and deterred those who seek to have a faith in God, something that is almost totally unforgivable in God's eyes (see Matthew 18:6).

The list of sins is very long. In the end, like the Prodigal Son, we find ourselves standing before our own personal "pig trough" of failures and we know that we too need to come home. But this is where the analogy starts to break down. The Prodigal Son was, in many ways, better off than most of us. He actually came to his senses in time and realized that he needed to go home. Many of us, at best, only have begun to suspect that we need to make that U-turn and go home. Additionally, the son had a home to go back to, and apparently he knew how to get there. Today many of us do not know where home is any longer. We have allowed our churches and families to fall into disrepair physically, morally and spiritually.

This brings me to the main point I wish to make. After spending over 35 years as a CPA in public practice and seeing the kind of personal burdens people have saddled themselves with, I believe that many are beginning to come to their senses and will want to return home. But, as we have seen, in many cases they have no home to return to. These people will be returning after being away for many years. They have not been practicing and have forgotten the core basics of their faith. Many are hurt and have been abused. They have hurt and abused many people themselves. In short, they have been at war with their families, their jobs and society itself.

While our Father is still present and ready to accept them back, the support and resources these prodigals will require are no longer in place. They will need a temporary spiritual home where they can receive the love and care they need to get reconnected with God and those around them. Quite a few will also have physical needs due to addiction issues and financial woes.

The system I am proposing is for us to return to the faith model of the early church of 2000 years ago. When Jesus had finished His work here on earth, the church He started began to thrive on its own. This early church succeeded at a time when it should not have logically been able to do so. Before Jesus left our world, I believe He created the mechanical and spiritual structure we know as the early church for the purposes of building the faith and meeting the physical needs of the people. It was His plan, and it worked to develop the new faith system that became known as Christianity. We have our faith today because the early church model functioned as Jesus intended.

Think about it. When the church was young it had no buildings, no denominations and no real formal hierarchy of leadership. There were simply the Apostles and the believers. The church had no special vocabulary and no theological system of Canon law and rules. Members of this new church were a persecuted people. Believers could lose their lives for being a Christian in this period. The church had no New Testament, and getting copies of what we know as the Old Testament today was almost impossible. How did Christianity survive? How did it even make it through the beginning of first century?

While the Christians of the first century certainly did not have the resources we have, they did have three critical elements, which we still have today. They had the verbal Gospel of Jesus Christ, they had each other for love and support and they had the Holy Spirit. The difference between us and them is that they chose to use those three resources and to rely heavily on them, whereas today we have largely grown indifferent to the words of Christ, to one another, and His Holy Spirit.

We are struggling with the application and growth of our faith, even though we have many more resources, including the printed and translated Word of God, modern communications and technology, and the absence of persecution in many areas of the world. What, then, are we missing? We're missing conversion and community. Conversion comes from reading and understanding the Word of God and relying on His Holy Spirit.

Community comes from living out the Word of God among one another with the help of His Holy Spirit. Community will help us to help those who need help.

Today's younger folks are looking for proof that the faith system called Christianity really works. They ultimately make that judgment by observing those of us who attend church and call ourselves Christians, to see if we practice what we preach.

We must return to the early church model. The prodigals (Baby Boomers) desperately need to return home, but they cannot come back to church life as it is currently structured. While there may be some churches presently configured to work as Christ commanded, they are in the minority. Things have to change.

Jesus gave us two great commandments, to love God and one another. There are those who think that if they focus mainly on loving God, while devoting some of their attention to other people, they are home free. But this is not true. It's worth repeating what I wrote in chapter 11. In 1 John 4:20, the Scriptures tell us, *"If anyone says, 'I love God,' yet hates his brother, he is a liar. For anyone who does not love his brother, whom he has seen, cannot love God whom he has not seen. And He has given us this command: Whoever loves God must also love his brother.'"* These words effectively tell us what we need to focus on.

Additionally, in Matthew 5:43, Jesus tells us in no uncertain terms that we need to pray and care for those who we consider our enemies. He wants us to pay serious attention to the people we would not normally be drawn to as friends. Furthermore, in Matthew 25:31, Jesus again outlines how He will decide who goes to Heaven and who does not. His decision will be based on the amount of love and care we offer those around us, especially the ones who are the most needy and who we normally shy away from.

If you examine Christ's teachings, you'll find the same themes woven throughout all of them. These themes are found in the stories of the Good Samaritan, the Great Commission, the lost sheep, and that incredible dialogue Jesus had with Peter just before He returned to Heaven. He asked Peter three times if he loved Him. Each time Peter said yes and Jesus responded again with a plea for Peter (and us) to take care of His lambs. It doesn't take much to see the core concern of Christ's heart; it is us. Here are the verses:

> *When they had finished eating, Jesus said to Simon Peter, "Simon son of John, do you truly love me more than these?"*
> *"Yes, Lord," he said, "you know that I love you."*
> *Jesus said, "Feed my lambs."*
> *Again Jesus said, "Simon son of John, do you truly love me?"*
> *He answered, "Yes, Lord, you know that I love you."*
> *Jesus said, "Take care of my sheep."*
> *The third time he said to him, "Simon son of John, do you love me?"*
> *Peter was hurt because Jesus asked him the third time, "Do you love me?" He said, "Lord, you know all things; you know that I love you."*
> *Jesus said, "Feed my sheep."*　　　(John 21:15-18)

Jesus wants all of His children to come home to be with Him. We need to return to the model of the early church because it was the one established physically by Christ Himself and because it worked so effectively in the beginning. It is the only model that will now succeed. We've tried everything else since the first century and obviously our efforts have left much to be desired. What will the early church of the 21st century look like? Here is a list of the features of the early church as described by Michael Green in his book *Who is This Jesus?*

The early church consists of:

- people who know God and Jesus intimately, not just know about Him.
- people who want to glorify God, that is, they want to reflect Him to others who they encounter every day regardless of their surroundings at the time.
- people who will keep His word, that is, they observe and obey His teachings rather than try to find ways of circumventing its challenge.
- people who believe that Jesus came from God with a unique mission to save us from the power of sin and Hell.
- people who are united in purpose, mutual love and see us belonging to the same family.
- people who live their lives in the world along with all those around them. They do not seek to become hermit types, separating themselves from the group but people who want to show God's love to others. In short their goal is to help God in the rescue of lost souls.
- people who have the same sort of joy that Jesus displayed. Our job is to show those around us that a life in Christ is something to sing about.
- people who can endure whatever comes their way and to do it with the help of their brothers and sisters as well as the Holy Spirit.
- people who have realized that this earthly home is temporary. Our real permanent residence is not of this world.

It is beyond that border crossing we spoke of earlier.

- people who will not become involved in things that are clearly illegal or wrong. We must keep to the high road at all costs so we can show others the true way home.
- people who will not be comfortable just sitting in a church week after week thinking that just showing up on Sunday is all that needs to be done.
- people who will model the love Jesus has given them through the presence of His Holy Spirit. With God's Spirit flowing through them and out of them, many will be impacted for the Kingdom in a very practical manner, and the journey home will become much easier.

I listed these features so that we can get a better picture of what we need to become in order to re-establish the early church. These features also do a good job of describing the nature and purpose of the early church. Certainly, the details of how each early church model is developed and maintained will vary from place to place. But in every case, these models will be replicas of the original church in that they will operate as they did some 2000 years ago.

In this form of the early church, people will gather in a place and hear the Word of God. They will praise Him, and as the Holy Spirit enters their life, they will be anxious to show their love and concern for those around them. But this form of the early church will also, in a sense, be temporary. It is not meant to replace existing churches. I am not suggesting that we do away with things like the sacraments or established church law.

The early church model can only act as a center to help process and aid the prodigal son and daughter back to a certain level of health. Think of it as a spiritual clinic or hospital where people can go for emergency care, healing and the reacquisition of basic spiritual knowledge and teachings. Once their spiritual condition is stabilized, they can then become permanent members of an established church home.

However, if established churches do not embrace the core elements of the early church model, the entire process will fail and we will be worse off than we are now. All of the elements of current church practices will have to be measured in light of the early church of the first century. Remember, the early church worked even under extreme persecution. There will most likely be resistance to this movement from current established church leaders. They will not want to lose their power and position. All I'll say about this is that those people need to read and reread Matthew chapter 23. Jesus' harshest words were for the church leaders of His day as you will see below.

Let's take another step forward. There is a piece of Scripture that has recently received much attention in the Christian world. In this verse from the Old Testament, God is speaking to His people because they have strayed far from His laws. Yet He offers them a way to restore their land and redeem their lives with Him:

> *If my people, who are called by my name, will humble themselves and pray and seek my face and turn from their wicked ways, then will I hear from heaven and will forgive their sin and will heal their land.*

(2 Chronicles 7:14)

This verse is very easily misunderstood. In it, God appears to be explaining that if the people repent and turn from their evil ways, He will put things back in order and He will restore the fruitfulness of their lands. But this is not so. First of all, He is speaking to *His* people, the ones that call themselves, in today's terms, Christians. He is not addressing those who do not believe in Him.

Secondly, He is admonishing us "believers" for adopting sinful lifestyles. In other words, it is up to us to make the U-turn first. The rest of the world is looking to us for answers and a way to live correctly. If those around us do not find answers to these questions by observing our lifestyles, then they will not find it anywhere else, and consequently, they very well could be lost in the end.

God knows all of this and therefore He is very concerned that we make the necessary changes. We who consider ourselves followers of Christ need to make the U-turn. But equally urgent is the need for our Christian churches to realize that they too are on the wrong path. The church, as a whole, needs to make a giant U-turn. For the Catholic Church, that U-turn was started some 35 years ago with the Charismatic movement. But as people got closer and closer to God on a personal level, the Church hierarchy began to shut down the Charismatic services and the movement itself. Now we, both as individuals and the church at large, desperately need to make a U-turn; I only hope we have enough time and courage to do so.

As for us today, look at how blessed we are in this country of ours. Many of us in America, according to our own rating standards, are considered to be the wealthiest people in the whole world! What excuse do we have for not living as God has told us to live? The following two verses make this point painfully clear.

*That servant who knows his master's will and does not get ready or does not do what his master wants will be beaten with many blows. But the one who does not know and does things deserving punishment will be beaten with few blows. From everyone who has been given much, much will be demanded; and from the one who has been entrusted with much, much more will be asked.* (Luke 12:47-48)

Let's go even further; this next point is so very important. In the 23rd chapter of Matthew, Jesus does something unbelievable: He criticizes the Pharisees, and he does so in no uncertain terms. These were the religious leaders of the day, the equivalent of our modern day bishops, cardinals, priests, ministers and church hierarchy. Here's a portion of what He said to them:

*Woe to you, teachers of the law and Pharisees, you hypocrites! You shut the kingdom of heaven in men's faces. You yourselves do not enter, nor will you let those enter who are trying to.*
*Woe to you, teachers of the law and Pharisees, you hypocrites! You travel over land and sea to win a single convert, and when he becomes one, you make him twice as much a son of hell as you are.*
*Woe to you, teachers of the law and Pharisees, you hypocrites! You give a tenth of your spices — mint, dill and cumin. But you have neglected the more important matters of the law — justice, mercy and faithfulness. You should have practiced the latter, without neglecting the former.* (Matt 23:13-15, 23)

You have to remember, Jesus did not speak this way in the Gospels to anyone else. These are very harsh words, particularly when you consider that He was addressing the leaders of the church in the presence of many people. But He was angry, and His anger was justified. The Pharisees and other religious leaders were doing very little to help their people find God, but instead were burdening people with a multitude of man-made laws and making their lives harder.

The Pharisees did practice the strict letter of the law. In effect, however, they preserved the good life for themselves, while being guilty of hypocrisy and other offenses. The new early church of the 21st century will have to think and act exactly as Jesus did some two thousand years ago. It will also have to beware that it does not become guilty of the same behavior as the Pharisees.

Let me remind you of a story I spoke of earlier, because it truly encapsulates one of the most important truths we need to understand now. Think of the world as being divided up into three parts. On one side we have the true believers; on the opposite side we have the non-believers. In between those two groups, in the vast middle ground that exists, we have the *make-believers*. Who are the make-believers?

*We* will be make believers if:

- we continue to think that all of our problems today are nothing new, that every generation experiences them, and we shouldn't get too worried about it, or that it's just the way the world works today and there's not much you can do about it;
- we continue to make believe that our current way of living will eventually work out fine and that there is no need for a major change in our thinking or our actions;
- we continue to think that our present heading may take us a bit out of the way from where we want to be

in life, but in the end everything will work out just fine;

- we continue to make believe that our children will figure out right from wrong on their own and that they really do not need a lot of our help and advice;
- we continue to think that our children do not watch us and learn more from our actions than from what we say to them;
- we continue to think that the old ways of doing things just do not relate to the challenges we meet in life today, so we can forget about those ways since they are irrelevant;
- we continue to allow all these kinds of things to continue and then think that our spiritual debt to God and our sin in His eyes will not condemn us;
- we ignore the messages of the Old and New Testament writers and that of Christ Himself which tell us to repent, to change our thinking and ways and to follow God's ways.

*Jesus Christ is the same yesterday and today and forever.*
(Hebrews 13:8)

And finally, there is a place in the gospel of John where Jesus does something very unusual.

*Some time later, Jesus went up to Jerusalem for a feast of the Jews. Now there is in Jerusalem near the Sheep Gate a pool, which in Aramaic is called Bethesda and which is surrounded by five covered colonnades. Here a great number of disabled people used to lie — the blind, the lame, the paralyzed. One who was there had been an invalid for thirty-eight years. When Jesus saw him lying there and learned that he had been in this condition for a long time, he asked him, "Do you want to get well?"*

*"Sir," the invalid replied, "I have no one to help me into the pool when the water is stirred. While I am trying to get in, someone else goes down ahead of me."*

*Then Jesus said to him, "Get up! Pick up your mat and walk." At once the man was cured; he picked up his mat and walked.*

*The day on which this took place was a Sabbath, and so the Jews said to the man who had been healed, "It is the Sabbath; the law forbids you to carry your mat."*

*But he replied, "The man who made me well said to me, 'Pick up your mat and walk.'"*

*So they asked him, "Who is this fellow who told you to pick it up and walk?"*

*The man who was healed had no idea who it was, for Jesus had slipped away into the crowd that was there. Later, Jesus found him at the temple and said to him, <u>"See, you are well again. Stop sinning or something worse may happen to you."</u> The man went away and told the Jews that it was Jesus who had made him well.*

(John 5:1-15 emphasis added)

This passage may be difficult for us to understand. Why would Jesus heal a person who had been sick and crippled for over 38 years and then warn him that he might have even more trouble in the future? It seems as if Jesus is purposely trying to devalue the man's miraculous recovery and personal joy.

I believe that the message from this short story is enormous for us today. Anyone who has been seriously ill or in trouble, to the point where their very lives and all that they have is threatened, knows the joy and the intense sense of relief they feel when the worst does not happen to them. They can leave the courtroom, the hospital or scene of the accident a free person, a healed person and an unharmed person. But we also know what happens to them the very next day; they have the option of doing things that could get them into even more trouble. This is an all-too-familiar routine for the alcoholic that returns to the bottle time and again, or the offender who violates his probation and is now in even more trouble.

Jesus was telling this man that even though he was healed from his physical ailment, he needed an even greater miracle. He needed to have his sins forgiven. He needed to change his way of thinking and acting, to confess his sins and to move off in a new and corrected direction. In other words, he needed to make a U-turn.

*And this is the lesson we need to learn today. Many of us in the Baby Boomer generation are like that crippled man. Perhaps we are even more debilitated than him because we have been indulging in a wide variety of bad behavior for even longer than 38 years. And now we can see clearly the resulting consequences for our society, families and businesses. Yes, we can be healed by God, but if we do not change our thinking, our heading and our actions, then something worse may—and probably will—happen to us. We have to stop being make-believers.*

I don't think there can be any greater sin than that of misleading ourselves and our children away from God. The fact is that our children and those closest to us need to know for certain that the way we are leading them is the correct way. Just as they need to know that they will have air to breathe, food to eat, clothing, money, homes and jobs, they also need to know that they will be loved by us and by God. They need to know God on a personal level. They need to find Him and their way home in the end.

Make no mistake about it.

We need to make a U-turn in our lives.

We've waited until the eleventh hour.

Will you turn and change your ways... or not?

*"The hero is one who kindles a great light in the world, who sets up blazing torches in the dark streets of life for men to see by. The saint is the man who walks through the dark paths of the world, himself a light."*

~ Felix Adler (1851-1933);
intellectual, founder of the Society for Ethical Culture

# Epilogue:
# A Modern-Day Conversation with Jesus

*"There are two ways of spreading light: to be the candle or the mirror that reflects it."*

~ Edith Wharton (1862-1937);
American novelist

**P:** Good morning Lord.

**J:** Hello Paul. I'm very glad we have this chance to talk.

**P:** Yes, thank You for the opportunity, Lord. There's so much I want to ask You, but right now all of the big questions I had for You seem to escape me.

**J:** (He laughs) Well, let Me help you out, Paul. You have just written a book and are wondering if you are on the right track in what you are telling people. Am I correct?

**P:** Yes, that's a great place to start and I am most definitely concerned about that question.

**J:** Well one thing's for sure; you've got so much Scripture in the book that you have to be on the right track! You know, all throughout the history of the world, the very thing that always managed to bring down civilization after civilization was man's inability to really care about one another. With some societies in the past We've seen periods of great peace and progress but then repeatedly, evil would enter the picture usually in some form of hatred and greed, and destroy all the progress. It's been the greatest disappointment to Us ever since We created the first humans (Genesis 6:5).

Many found out very late in life that they were headed in the wrong direction and gave up in trying to make that U-turn you speak of in your book. If more people had thought about doing that, We would have moved to help them in returning to what they knew was the right thing to do in their lives. As it was, those that chose to reject Our help continued on the wrong road and it ended up destroying their lives. So your book is exactly the kind of message that We are most concerned about: the return of all the prodigals and we hope that they will "see the light" in time.

**P:** Who is "Us" and "We," Lord?

**J:** I'm referring to My Father, Myself and the Holy Spirit. You know, the Trinity.

**P:** Oh yes, of course. But since you brought it up, I've always wanted to know why You bothered to make us in the first place? Didn't You know ahead of time that man would fail to live up to your expectations?

**J:** Yes, my Father knew that all along. But you have to understand something about Us. As the Trinity, We are the essence of love. At the fundamental core of love is a giving and receiving of the things that love brings to a relationship. You cannot have true love unless both parties freely and willingly choose to share that love. It's as if both persons desire to pour themselves out into each other, over and over, back and forth, and always long to be together to enjoy that process.

We are the same way and We need others to share our love with forever. So We created man and woman to be immortal but We had to give each one a free will to do what they really desired. Without that free will, they would become like the rest of creation, subject to instinct and in a sense, pre-programmed to respond positively to Our love. It had to be different with human beings. We had to give them the option to reject Our love, otherwise whatever developed between Us wouldn't and couldn't be true love.

**P:** I think I understand. But before we get back to the issue of my book, I've always wondered about something else. Before man ever sinned against you, where did the snake come from in the Garden of Eden? The Garden was supposed to be a paradise, undefiled and not subject to the influences of evil, was it not? Why would you let the snake, which we now know was Satan, into the Garden?

**J:** Once again, Adam and Eve, being the first created people, needed to have a choice. Without the snake, there could be no real way to choose love over evil, Us over Satan. Besides, We had the same issue with the angels when We made them. We gave them the ability to choose as well, and, as you know, some decided to not love Us. Lucifer was the biggest disappointment to Us. He decided to represent, and in fact become, the actual embodiment of all that was and is the opposite of Us. Whatever We are not, he is.

**P:** So you knew that some would reject your love even before you made them? Well then, I guess that really answers my big question about the existence of Heaven and Hell. They are real places aren't they?

**J:** Yes, they are real. You see, to put it in terms you can understand, We live in Heaven where love is all there is and the expression and content of the love relationships found in Heaven affects everyone there. Being in a place where everyone really loves one another is unimaginable for you. The love relationship between each person and Us feeds on one another and becomes even greater. It is literally an incredible experience. But then there has to be a place for all of those who reject the concept of true love. Creating Hell was not done out of spite or retribution but rather as a way to keep Heaven pure.

Once We created people and gave them the ability to choose for themselves, then there had to be a place that would accommodate the consequences of either choice. Hence you have Heaven and Hell. People are given a lifetime on earth to make their choice as to where they want to spend eternity. We made each person with their own free will and We will always honor the choices they make. No one will be brought to Heaven against their will. But many in the end will greatly regret choosing Hell as did that rich man in the story about Lazarus the beggar (Luke 16:19). Oh, in the end, when some people find out that they will not be going to Heaven, they will be extremely sorry. But that's why We have given every-one a lifetime to make the choice. If you wait until the end, it will most probably be too late.

**P:** Yes, but I think if people really understood the true conse-quences of their actions they would not choose Hell. Lots of people just cannot believe that there would be a place like Hell, and, for all eternity no less. As you know that is why I decided to write this book. It seems to me that people have to wake up and turn around. It seems that we're on the wrong road and headed for tremendous destruction (See Matthew 7:13-14).

**J:** I know, I know, you are correct. Satan has been hard at work to convince many people that the way they are living is okay and that everything will work out in the end. What they are not being told is the truth. It is absolutely critical to under-stand that things just *are* as they are. People think that as the Trinity We can simply snap our fingers and make any-thing change as the need arises. It does not work that way. Look at all of nature. It has worked as it does today for all the years since We created the world and the universe. Even the three of Us *are* a certain way. We were not created. We just are as We are. That is where many people make their biggest mistake. They think that they have a "license to sin," if you will. And they feel that in the end, despite all of their unconfessed sin, that We will relent and make an exception to the rules just for them alone. It will not be that way. As for informing people better about the truth of this matter, you now have the Internet, and many versions of the Scrip-tures, the Church, clergy etc. In many ways the world today has no excuse. You cannot claim ignorance of the truth.

Never before in all of history have people had more opportunity to find out the truth about the Christian faith and Us. I came to earth in the flesh once and many did not believe Me. If I returned to earth once more, the result would still be the same. Even I could not prove beyond a doubt the truth found in the Scriptures. I could work all kinds of miracles but once again it is up to each person to choose to believe what they hear and see. And similarly they have to choose for themselves to make that U-turn as well. No one can force them. You folks have a saying... you can lead a horse to water but you cannot make him drink.

P: Yes, I can believe all of that, but what is it about us that prevents us from believing? What is it that keeps us from making that U-turn, turning back to find the right road and following it even when we know, or at least suspect, that we are currently headed in the wrong direction?

J: Your free will is a very powerful force, Paul. Actually, in a sense, it is the most powerful force in the universe even more powerful than Us. Why? Because We have to honor it. We cannot trump your free will. You are in fact in control of your own destiny in that regard. So, you have that fact as being true and the additional fact that nowadays your society has an incredible amount of access to worldly pleasures and things. And many of those things distract people and contribute to their losing sight of what is true and important. Consumerism has taken hold of your culture, especially those societies in the developed countries. You have financial credit available, you have all kinds of desirable things accessible for purchase, there are unprecedented levels of temptation, and then there's your free will. It's like the perfect storm for causing people to sin.

For many it's too much to resist. Plus the Christian church has lost much of its influence and is largely ignored by many, especially the young folks. And by the way, that last part is what is going to condemn many of your generation (Matthew 18:6). It's not so much what people *are doing* for their children but rather what they are *not doing* for and with them. Once people have their way, they become invested and comfortable in their lives and much of it can be sin ridden. They then find themselves in bondage to that way of life and become slaves to it. It's very similar to becoming addicted to any substance. Their children get hurt by having to grow up in that same environment. It pollutes their minds, bodies and spirits.

**P:** Wow... well then, what do you think of this U-turn concept I've been talking about in my book? Does it really have value and does it make any sense to you?

**J:** Of course it makes sense... I'm the one that planted it in your brain to begin with!

**P:** Oh, okay, but could You please elaborate a bit more for the folks reading this?

**J:** Yes, I'd love to. By now you realize that there will be a judgment day sometime in the future. It is a day designed to separate the "wheat from the chaff" (Matthew 3:11-12 and Matthew 25:31). It has to be this way in order to preserve all that is already established in Heaven. Remember, Heaven was never created. Just like Us, it is a place or state of being that just *is*. Anything sinful or soiled by sin just cannot exist there. It would be impossible to allow it in. It would be like having cold and hot existing at the same time and in the exact same place. They are mutually exclusive. One is the opposite of the other.

That being said, We are most interested in people desiring to return to the love relationship that their Father offers. What you call a U-turn is really another way of saying "repent." People need a change in their thinking which will then prompt the U-turn in their actions. It is just like in the story I told about the Prodigal Son. He was indeed lost and gone forever until he decided to make a U-turn. He left his father. He took his inheritance prematurely. He used his free will to choose what he wanted and he chose to be away from his father's love. So whenever anyone wants to come back and reverse their original decision, We are most joyous. All of Heaven rejoices as well because that decision is so important. It is a decision that affects them forever. (Luke 15:10)

**P:** Well, this is what worries me Lord. What you say makes sense to me now but it seems many will go to their graves not understanding the truth about all of this. What can be done about it?

**J:** Yes, most regrettably you are correct. Many people have already died without turning to the Father's love. Once again, it is what it is. That is the cost of free will; the right to choose for yourself. But once again you have asked the same question as the one asked by the rich man in the story of Lazarus the beggar (see Luke 16:19) and many others over the years. He was wealthy and repeatedly turned against the love of my Father. His greed got the best of him. After he died and was in a place of torment, he realized his folly but it was all too late and he wanted Us to do something about it. He wanted Us to alert his family and friends who were still alive. We told him that those who are still alive have the Scriptures, the message of the prophets and the Commandments given to Moses to help guide them. That is enough for them if they really are interested in learning the truth. And it is even truer today with all of the information you now have at your fingertips.

**P:** Then the last day will be both a day of great sorrow and joy, will it not?

**J:** Yes, it will be unlike anything anyone could even begin to imagine (Matthew 25:31). But let me give you some hope here. My Holy Spirit is at work throughout the world constantly prodding and intervening for people. You remember the story of the thief that was crucified with Me on the cross. He waited until the last minute to come home and in the end he did make the right choice. You would be surprised how many others over the course of history have died that way. But then again, the other thief did not take my offer to be in Paradise; so be it. That was his choice.

You see, earth is a temporary place. The entire universe was created by Us long ago. Everything in the universe is subject to time and space and will eventually pass away or at least the earth as you know it will pass away. Since time and space have no meaning in all of eternity, the world We are from is very different than yours. But something absolutely unbelievable occurred some 2000 years ago. My Father allowed something in your temporal world to occur that would affect the eternal world. My death was that event. My Father could not bear to see all of His creation spend eternity without Him in Hell. So by my cross and resurrection, people once again have the choice of going to Heaven or not. But again it is still a choice. No one will go there automatically.

My personal sacrifice opened the door that was shut to all mankind since Adam and Eve first sinned. So there are basically two choices that people have to make. It is either Heaven or Hell. The real problem is that the latter option has no possibility of parole and many do not want to believe that.

**P:** Jesus, please tell us about the early church after You left to go back to Heaven. I brought that up in my book and I hope I was correct in using that period of time as a model for us to follow.

**J:** Yes, you could not have chosen a better model to follow. Many did leave Me when I was taken away to be crucified. In a way, I cannot blame them. They saw Me as their invincible leader. They just never thought I would die. Just days before My death when they took all of those palm branches and placed them on the path for Me as we entered Jerusalem, My heart went out to all of them. They simply had no idea of what was to come. And they were devastated when I was taken from them. But as you now know, it was something that had to be done. It was the main reason why I came to earth in the first place.

If you read John chapter 17, just before I died I was concerned for my followers. I knew My death would be a hard thing for them to overcome. So I prayed long and hard about it. But in the end they came through for Me and those around them. Very few historians have ever come to understand what those people went through after I left. But because of their tenacity in clinging to the truth I told them, they were blessed by My Holy Spirit in many ways but especially in the form of the growth of the Church. The Christian faith thrived in the first several hundred years after My death largely due to the prayers, sacrifices, commitments and outright martyrdom of My followers. Many made U-turns in their lives. Many gave up everything to continue to do what I, and the leaders of the early church, instructed them to do.

You know, if the people of your generation in the 21st century would wake up and realize that this is the right way to get home and started to act in a manner similar to the early church, I would bless them in ways beyond any of their imaginations. For all of the bad things that are currently happening in your society and world, all of Us working together could turn that around in a heartbeat! I know, I know, that sounds too good to be true but after all We are God and We did not create man to be living as he is now. You were designed and built to live glorious lives. And that can still become a reality. But people have to use their "trump cards" and want to make a U-turn as you put it in your book.

**P:** Oh wow... can I ask if you see them possibly responding this way in the near future?

**J:** Everything is possible with God's help but again the people have to want it wholeheartedly. Why? Because it will always cost a great deal to accomplish this work. To follow in My footsteps for example, is a very expensive undertaking. The reason is mainly because of our adversary Satan and his forces. Yes, he is real... very real. Unfortunately he is succeeding in convincing many in the world today that he is not real or that he is not that bad. He is also telling people that in the end, We will grant something like a sweeping clemency to all regardless of their sins and let everyone into Heaven. Again, We cannot do that. It is literally against Our nature and the plan of salvation that is already in place since time began. I died in order that Heaven might once again be *made available* to all who love the Father. If the plan was to automatically grant everyone access to Heaven in the end anyway, I would not have had to die on that cross. For that matter you wouldn't need churches, priests, prayers etc.

Whether many will see the light and do what those people did some 2000 years ago remains to be seen. The coming trials and period of tribulation that your generation will experience has been a long time in the making. This is like the Prodigal Son's time of deciding to make a U-turn. The Scriptures do not describe what it took for him to make it home again once he realized his mistake in leaving. Remember, he had no money, food or resources and he was a long way from home in a foreign land. The fact is that he barely made it back alive. He had an incredibly difficult time coming back home. But We helped him do it because We knew that in his heart he really wanted to make that U-turn.

It is the tough times that usually provide the deciding moment when people have to finally choose which road to take. It literally is up to each person to respond to Our love and help. It is available to all even up to the very moment of death. This has happened many times before on earth. However, with regard to your time now in the 21st century, it is very different only because never has there been so many people who have over-indulged themselves in so much sinful behavior even to the point of mass addiction. The amount of physical wealth alone that has been squandered by your generation is staggering even to Us here in Heaven! And so the stakes have never been higher. Your leaders and the people of your time have raised those stakes to be the highest ever in all of history. And the other thing that complicates the situation is the great numbers of needy people all over the world. In your time now, you have the ability, resources and mechanization to help many of those people. But still your generation refuses to accomplish it *to the degree* that you are capable of doing the task.

**P:** I was afraid this was the case all along. Where can we look in Scripture for guidance to our specific condition? Is there a special verse?

**J:** You know, Paul, there is a place in Revelation where I spoke about the conditions of a church in a place called Laodicea. Those people were like many of your generation today, wealthy, seemingly self sufficient, oblivious to the danger signs around them and indulging in everything that was available at the time. Their society was heavily laden with sin and debt just as yours is today. I wish I could give you more encouraging words right now but if I did, I would not be telling you the truth.

Here is what I said to those people through my prophet the apostle John:

*I know your deeds, that you are neither cold nor hot. I wish you were either one or the other! So, because you are lukewarm — neither hot nor cold — I am about to spit you out of my mouth. You say, "I am rich; I have acquired wealth and do not need a thing." But you do not realize that you are wretched, pitiful, poor, blind and naked. I counsel you to buy from me gold refined in the fire, so you can become rich; and white clothes to wear, so you can cover your shameful nakedness; and salve to put on your eyes, so you can see.*
*Those whom I love I rebuke and discipline. So be earnest, and repent. Here I am! I stand at the door and knock. If anyone hears my voice and opens the door, I will come in and eat with him, and he with me.*
*To him who overcomes, I will give the right to sit with me on my throne, just as I overcame and sat down with my Father on his throne. He, who has an ear, let him hear what the Spirit says to the churches.*

(Revelation 3:15-22)

**P:** Yes Lord, I remember those verses well. They are chilling to hear and they frighten me more than anything else. But specifically, what action is it that we must now take above all other things?

**J:** Let Me answer you this way. I grew up with Joseph and Mary as they were my earthly parents. As soon as I could, I began working with Joseph in his carpentry trade that was attached in a room to the side of our home. That workshop was so safe and secure for me. I was good at the work and many people sought me out for repairing their things.

Joseph died when I was still a teenager. I had to then carry the work and financial burden for the family, something I did for as long as I could.

But there came a day, Paul, when I knew I had to leave the security of that workshop. I knew I had to leave my mother and the safe position I had created for myself in my work. Believe it or not, I really struggled with that decision on a physical and human level. I knew what awaited Me in Jerusalem. I worked every day with hammers and nails. I knew what was coming and My body was very much afraid to leave.

I prayed to my Father about all of this and He strengthened me and when the day came that I knew I had to leave that shop, I was able to do it. The people of your generation and time have a similar choice to make now. Many are feeling safe and secure in how they are living. But that is a false sense of security. You are at great risk these days. You too must leave your "workshops" and move among the needy as I did. Specifically, you must do what they did in the early church some 2000 years ago. Go to people in need and help them. The only thing that will work now is "one on one" attention. The Good Samaritan did it that way, the apostles, saints and martyrs all did that and I did that for two or three years on my way to Jerusalem. I showed them the way to the cross and it is the path of perseverance, charity and love. That is what your people must do now. Time is running out for them Paul. Please continue to tell them this. We will continue to help you in this task.

But here's another word of caution for you. John, the Gospel writer, wrote about that conversation I had with the crippled man at the Pool of Bethesda. I did heal him but he then had to go and live his new life without getting caught in temptation or sin. Now that he was able to walk again, his free will would have access to more things. It was then possible for him to get himself into even more trouble. Similarly, when I fed the 5000 people with just a few loaves and a couple of fish, do you realize what happened to all those people the very next day?

**P:** Yes Lord, they were hungry again.

**J:** That's exactly right. You see, We are not going to interfere with man's free will. People will have to decide for themselves how they want to live day by day. There are all kinds of miracles that We send to people all the time. But they are not permanent cures for all eternity or that they provide automatic tickets to Heaven. However in a sense they can be. If people take the time to study them they will see where they came from and that very knowledge can show them the way home. The miracles are clues and signposts that will help people get home. But even after you have received one, there is more danger that you might let your guard down thinking that you are home free. That's when you can get into even more trouble.

But while certain ways of living will lead you home to be with Us, others can easily lead you away from Us. Paul, there is always hope. People just have to wake up to the truth of their situation. Once they do, We will help them turn things around and return home. Our Holy Spirit stands ready all the time, 24/7. So continue to promote the word that you have about repentance. Call it what you like, "U-turns" or some other phrase, but continue to help people see the light and make their way home. Nothing is more important than to find yourself on the inside of the gates of Heaven at the end of that last day. *Absolutely nothing is more important than that.*

**P:** Jesus, I want to thank You for taking the time to talk with me about these issues.

**J:** You are most welcome, of course. Just remember, I am always available to listen to what concerns you. My Holy Spirit is always working to help you. So just call on Me...We will be there. Let Me end this discussion with you as I did many years ago.

*All authority in heaven and on earth has been given to me. Therefore go and make disciples of all nations, baptizing them in the name of the Father and of the Son and of the Holy Spirit, and teaching them to obey everything I have commanded you. And surely I am with you always, to the very end of the age.*

(Matthew 28:18-20)

## The End

# *About the author and contact information*

Angelo Ramunni grew up as a Catholic on Long Island, New York in the 1950's and 60's. He attended Catholic schools all throughout his formal educational career. After he graduated from Fairfield University with a bachelor's degree in Economics in 1970, he went on to earn a Masters Degree in Economics from Fordham University and eventually a second Masters Degree in Accounting from Long Island University in 1976.

In 1978 he became a Certified Public Accountant and started his own public accounting firm in 1982, of which he is still a partner. His work with clients, both on a business and personal level, led him to focus on the larger issues concerning people's wealth and how they could best utilize their assets in a manner that would please God. Gradually he found himself talking to clients and friends more and more about spiritual matters as he analyzed peoples' needs and concerns about their future.

Over the years, Angelo became very active in his church and other para-church ministries such as FCCI, Fellowship of Companies for Christ Int'l (Christ at Work). He has also been involved in the Lions Club, Exchange Club, and is a past president of a local Rotary International Club. He has personally facilitated many Bible studies, Christian Business Owners group meetings, taught seminars and workshops concerning the Godly use of money for individuals and business owners, as well as teaching groups how to integrate their faith with their work.

Angelo is also an instructor-in-residence at the University of Connecticut in the area of accounting and financial literacy and has been a director of numerous non-profit organizations over the years. He is currently a member of the board of directors of The Connecticut Mutual Holding Company, a regional three bank holding company. He lives in Canaan, Connecticut with his wife and best friend Marcia. He has two grown children, Daniel and Joy, his son-in-law Joseph and an incredible grandson, Joey.

It was early in 1990 when, because of his wife's prayers,

Angelo's life changed dramatically as he met Jesus Christ after having read a little book called In His Steps by Charles Sheldon. Her prayers made his ensuing walk with God possible and ultimately are responsible for the production of his books, *The Poor Catholic; The Road to Grace* self published by Grace Path Publications LLC in 2004 and *Left Turn, Right Turn, U-Turn* published by Xulon Press in 2011.

**Contact Info:**
**Email: ramunni@comcast.net**
**Phone: 860-833-1374**